PIE!

100 GORGEOUSLY GLORIOUS RECIPES

First published in Great Britain in 2014 by Absolute Press, an imprint of Bloomsbury Publishing Plc

Absolute Press
Scarborough House
29 James Street West
Bath BA1 2BT
Phone 44 (0) 1225 316013
Fax 44 (0) 1225 445836
E-mail office@absolutepress.co.uk
Website www.absolutepress.co.uk

Publisher Jon Croft
Commissioning Editor Meg Avent
Art Direction and Design Matt Inwood
Project Editor Alice Gibbs
Editor Anne Sheasby
Photography Mike Cooper
Food Styling Genevieve Taylor

ISBN: 9781472905666

Printed and bound in China by C&C Printing.

Bloomsbury Publishing Plc
50 Bedford Square
London WC1B 3DP
www.bloomsbury.com

A note about the text
This book was set using ITC Century and Serifa. The first Century typeface was cut in 1894. In 1975, an updated family of Century typefaces was designed by Tony Stan for ITC. The Serifa font was designed by Adrian Frutiger in 1978.

Thanks
Pie! has been a brilliant book to write and I have loved every minute of it. Most of the recipe testing happened during the hottest summer for many a year, yet funnily enough I received not one complaint from friends and family as I fed them endless pies in the blistering sun of the heatwave... proving there is a pie for everyone, whatever the weather. I'd like to say thanks, once again, to Absolute Press for trusting me with this book – Jon Croft, Meg Avent, Alice Gibbs and Matt Inwood – thank you one and all, it's always a pleasure.
Anne Sheasby, my editor, gets a massive thank you for doing such a thorough job ironing out all of the creases from my writing. Anne: your diligence is much appreciated!

Big thanks to Kate Hordern, my agent, for her consistently calm encouragement and positivity.

Photographer Mike Cooper yet again delivered a book full of beautiful images that are an inspiration. Thanks, Mike, for bringing my recipes alive!

Finally, thanks to my family, who make the endless multi-tasking that every working mum knows only too well feel not only possible but truly worth it.
Rob, Izaac and Eve: lots of love, always.

PIE!

100 GORGEOUSLY GLORIOUS RECIPES

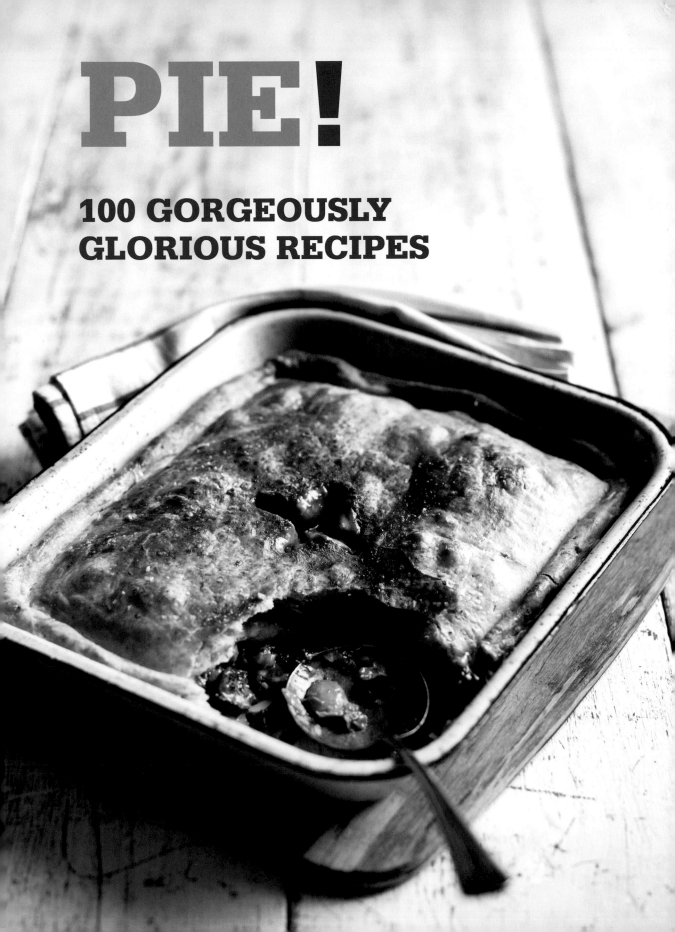

Caramelised Pear, Walnut and Gorgonzola Tarts, page 110

If there is a person in the land who doesn't enjoy a pie, then I certainly haven't met them! Universally adored, when you mention the word pie to almost anyone, the response is a simple and resounding 'mmmm'.

We all love to eat them, but pies are also wonderful things to cook for your loved ones, bringing you much well-earned praise, and isn't that just what all cooks desire and deserve?

Pies are firmly at the hands-on end of the cooking spectrum. Pastry is carefully made, flour is lightly dusted over the work surface, then the pastry is gently rolled and draped into the tin, and finally there is the art of cutting, shaping and decorating the pastry, not forgetting the all-important filling, of course. None of these stages are necessarily time-consuming or difficult, but they do simply need to be made from the heart.

Imagine a pie and invariably it'll be a pastry-topped version, either bursting with sweet fruit or a combination of tender meat and vegetables. Happily, however, we can stretch and mould the definition of a pie to include those ones topped with fluffy butter-rich mashed potato, or others, such as tarts or quiches, with pastry only on the bottom. Not to mention pasties, pork pies, samosas and turnovers, and even a pie made from pasta. From humble to luxurious creations, and super quick to satisfyingly time-consuming recipes, in Pie! you'll find them all, both savoury and sweet. Indeed, a glorious pie for every occasion you care to think of.

Happy baking!

**Genevieve Taylor
Bristol, September 2013**

Types of Pastry

There are three principle types of pastry that are used time and again throughout this book and they are shortcrust, rough puff pastry and true puff pastry. In this section, you will find basic recipes for shortcrust and rough puff pastry, along with a few flavour variations for each. But you will find no recipe for true puff pastry, as it's just way too elaborate and time-consuming to make in the home kitchen and is not something I would ever attempt. Ready-made puff pastry is perfectly acceptable, and if you stretch to the all-butter puff pastry (and I suggest you do, as eating pastry is a once in a while treat that should be savoured), then it is simply delicious. I tend to buy all-butter puff pastry (to my mind, if you're having puff pastry, you may as well have the proper stuff), so although recipes don't specify this, I would recommend using it if you can. I also include a basic recipe for hot water crust pastry in this section, as well as a couple of basic gluten-free pastry recipes a bit further on.

Ready-made Pastry

There is a good range of ready-made pastries available and they are a pretty good substitute for homemade pastry. Many are available as blocks or ready-rolled sheets and can be bought chilled or frozen, but the pack sizes do vary a bit. All-butter varieties provide the best flavour. Pretty much all shop-bought pastries are suitable for vegetarians, and many are also suitable for vegans, although all-butter pastries (and sometimes sweet shortcrust pastry) contain butter and are therefore not vegan.

Standard pack sizes for blocks of puff and shortcrust pastry tend to be 500g (though they sometimes vary between the fresh and frozen types). Ready-rolled sheets of puff pastry can vary a little from brand to brand, but in my recipes I tend to opt for a rectangular sheet from a 320g pack. Blocks of all-butter puff pastry tend to come in two pack sizes (500g or 375g packs, depending on whether you choose frozen or fresh). Ready-rolled all-butter puff pastry sheets, and ready-rolled shortcrust pastry sheets or rounds, are commonly available. All-butter shortcrust pastry is generally obtainable in blocks and ready-rolled sheets. Sweet shortcrust pastry (including all-butter varieties) is usually available as blocks or sheets. Lighter versions of puff and shortcrust pastry, as well as flavoured puff pastry, are sometimes obtainable. Chilled and frozen filo pastry is also readily available.

Filo Pastry

Filo is another pastry that personally I would never attempt to make and ready-made filo is very acceptable. When working with filo, remember that the thin sheets dry out very easily and they will then become very hard and brittle to work with, so keep the sheets you are not working with loosely covered with a clean damp tea towel. Warka (also known as warkha, warqa or brik pastry) is a type of North African filo-type pastry that is super-thin and is traditionally used in dishes such as Brik à l'oeuf (see page 114), but it can be hard to source so I normally use filo in its place. If you want to find real warka, it's worth trying to hunt it out in Middle Eastern shops, specialist North African stores or online.

Making Your Own Pastry

Which Fat is Best to Use?

For both shortcrust and rough puff pastry, I always use just butter as the principle fat. The exception to this rule is in the Hot Water Crust Pastry (see page 8) used in the Traditional Pork Pie and Raised Game Pie recipes (see pages 34 and 100 respectively), which uses half butter and half lard. Whilst lard or vegetable shortening do add more 'shortness' (basically crumbliness), I simply prefer the taste of all-butter pastry.

Water

When adding water to bind the fat and flour in pastry, the simple rule is the colder the better, which is why I specify ice-cold water. In the depths of winter, cold water straight from the tap should be OK, but in warmer months, I add a couple of ice cubes to a glass of cold water and let it chill down for a few minutes before using.

Shortcrust Pastry

Shortcrust is the simplest and most versatile of all pastries, and at its crumbly, crispest best it is delicious, but it can become a little tough and chewy if it's overworked. The best pastry is made as quickly as possible with the minimum of handling. The basic ratio is half fat to flour, and whilst my recipe below uses 180g flour to 90g butter, the recipe can easily be scaled up or down to suit.

There are two main ways to make shortcrust pastry, the traditional rubbing-in (by hand) method that I learnt years ago from my mum, or the much faster and easier food processor method, which is how I make it most of the time these days. With a little care I think it is perfectly possible to make pastry in a food processor that is just as delicious as the handmade stuff. However, because food processors are so fast and efficient, there can be a tendency to over-process the dough, giving a tough and dense pastry, so just bear this in mind.

This is the basic quantity of shortcrust pastry I use to make pies, and one batch is enough to line a deep or shallow 25cm tart tin or 6 individual tartlet tins (each about 10cm diameter and 2cm deep) or 4 slightly larger ones (each about 12cm diameter and 3cm deep). A single batch is also enough for a single-crust pie top/lid. For double-crust pies, simply double the ingredient quantities to make a double batch of the basic pastry.

Makes about 325g | Takes 10 minutes to make (plus chilling)

180g plain white flour
a pinch of fine salt
90g cold butter, cut into small cubes
3–4 tbsp ice-cold water

Food Processor Method

Put the flour and salt into the food processor and whizz briefly together to mix, then add the butter cubes and pulse briefly a dozen times or so until you have coarse crumbs. If you use the pulse function in very short, sharp bursts (rather than just leave it in the 'on' position) to rub the fat and flour together, then I think it works more like super fast fingers and there is less chance of overdoing it. Next, you trickle in the ice-cold water, whilst pulsing all the while, just until the mixture resembles rough lumps and looks a bit like overcooked and dry scrambled eggs. Add only as much water as you need. Don't keep processing until the mixture comes together in a big ball as that will develop the gluten in the flour too much, so be sure to stop before you get to that stage.

Tip the clumped crumbs onto a sheet of cling film and gently squeeze together into a ball without pressing too hard – little air gaps are a good thing and will add a lightness and crumbliness to the cooked shortcrust. Wrap and chill in the fridge for at least 30 minutes before rolling out.

Traditional Rubbing-in (by hand) Method

The method is essentially the same, but your fingertips and thumbs work together to literally rub the flour, salt and butter together until you have coarse crumbs. Lifting your hands out of the bowl as you rub adds air. Then once again, add just enough cold water to bring the mixture together into clumps – I find a blunt table knife is best to use here, using it to stir and cut through the crumbed mixture as you mix. Again, tip the clumped crumbs onto a sheet of cling film and squeeze gently into a ball, then wrap and chill in the fridge for at least 30 minutes before rolling out.

Flavoured Shortcrust Pastry

Sweet Shortcrust Pastry (Makes about 350g)

Add 25g icing sugar to the combined flour and butter crumbs and pulse briefly, before you add the water. To enrich even further – great for French-style patisserie tarts – add an egg yolk to the crumbed mix before you add the water. You will need a little less water (perhaps half) as the yolk adds liquid.

Parmesan Shortcrust Pastry (Makes about 350g)

Add 25g finely grated fresh Parmesan cheese to the combined flour and butter crumbs and pulse briefly, before you add the water.

Walnut Shortcrust Pastry (Makes about 365g)

In a food processor, blitz 40g walnuts until finely ground, then add the flour and salt and continue as per the basic shortcrust pastry recipe.

Rye or Wholemeal Shortcrust Pastry (Makes about 340g)

Simply follow the basic shortcrust pastry recipe, but replace half (90g) of the white flour with 90g plain wholemeal or rye flour. You may need to add a touch more water (an extra tablespoon or so) as the wholemeal and rye flours will absorb more water.

Rough Puff Pastry

Rough puff pastry is a cheat's puff pastry. It's not quite as rich and flaky as true puff pastry and it won't rise as much, but it is more flaky and layered than shortcrust pastry. Rough puff pastry has a slightly higher fat content than shortcrust pastry, but far less than true puff, which can be as rich as equal parts fat to flour.

With rough puff pastry, you are rolling together layers of fat and flour, then as the fat melts in the oven, the pastry separates into even layers. I have to say, whilst I would rarely consider making shortcrust by hand when I have a food processor to do the job for me, I do really enjoy the rhythm of rolling and turning, rolling and turning, that is involved when making rough puff pastry. Perhaps the beauty of it for me is the way you can so easily flavour it with herbs, spices and cheese.

Makes about 545g | Takes 25 minutes to make (plus chilling)

250g plain white flour, plus extra for dusting
a pinch of fine salt
175g cold butter, cut into 1cm dice
about 8 tbsp ice-cold water

Stir the flour and salt together in a large bowl. Toss through the diced butter until each cube is coated. Add just enough ice-cold water to bring it together to form a firm dough that is not too sticky – a metal spoon is the best tool for this job. There should be no loose pieces of fat or flour left in the bowl.

Turn the pastry out onto a lightly floured work surface and roll into a rough rectangle, about 1cm thick. With a short edge nearest to you, fold the top third down towards you into the middle, and then fold the bottom third up over it – just like folding a letter. Give the pastry a quarter turn (turn it 90 degrees) so that the folded edges are at the sides, then roll out to a rectangle again (same size as before) and repeat the folding. Repeat this turning, rolling and folding process 5 more times, keeping the work surface and rolling pin lightly floured. If it is a warm day or you're working in a particularly hot kitchen, you will need to chill the pastry in the fridge for 30 minutes halfway through the rolling and folding process. This will re-solidify the butter, otherwise it will start to melt. If it's a cool day, then I normally complete the rolling and folding process in one go, working as quickly as possible. Wrap the pastry in cling film and chill in the fridge for at least 1 hour before using.

Flavoured Rough Puff Pastry

Herby Rough Puff Pastry (makes about 545g)
Stir 1 teaspoon dried mixed herbs through the flour and salt, before adding the butter, then continue as per the basic rough puff pastry recipe.

Parmesan and Sage Rough Puff Pastry (Makes about 575g)
Stir 25g finely grated fresh Parmesan cheese and 8–10 finely chopped fresh sage leaves through the flour and salt, before adding the butter, then continue as per the basic rough puff pastry recipe.

Sweet Rough Puff Pastry (Makes about 585g)
Stir 3 tablespoons icing sugar through the flour and salt, before adding the butter, then continue as per the basic rough puff pastry recipe. For Cinnamon Rough Puff Pastry, add a teaspoon or so of ground cinnamon with the icing sugar – this pastry is a good one to use for an apple pie.

Hot Water Crust Pastry

This is the sturdy pastry used to make the Traditional Pork Pie (see page 34) and Raised Game Pie (see page 100). With no rubbing in of fat and no rolling out, it's a really easy pastry to make, just make sure you cut the fat into dice so it melts quickly as the water comes to the boil – if the fat lumps are big, they take too long to melt and the water can evaporate too much.

Makes about 595g | Takes 10 minutes to make (plus chilling)

300g plain white flour
1 tsp fine salt
1 egg
110ml cold water
60g lard, cut into 1cm dice
60g butter, cut into 1cm dice

Measure the flour into a mixing bowl and stir through the salt. Make a well in the centre and crack in the egg, then use the empty shell to flick a little of the flour over the surface of the egg so it is hidden. Put the measured cold water and the lard and butter into a small saucepan and set over a medium heat. Stir until the fats melt and the water is just coming up to the boil, then remove from the heat and pour this hot mixture over the flour and egg in the bowl. Mix continuously with a metal spoon until the mixture comes together as a ball.

Tip onto the work surface and knead briefly for a minute or so, then wrap tightly in cling film, forming it into a fat sausage shape as you wrap. Chill in the fridge for 30–45 minutes to firm up before using, but don't over-chill or it will become very hard to work with.

Rolling Out the Pastry and Lining Your Tin

Whether you are rolling shortcrust, puff or rough puff pastry, a little flour dusted over the work surface is essential, but too much will dry out the pastry, so just dust over as much as you need, remembering you can always add more.

Rolling pastry is so much easier if you start with the rough shape you want to finish with, so if you need a big circle, start by pressing your ball of pastry into a thick circular shape before you begin to roll. To keep it circular, roll no more than 2 or 3 times in one direction, before turning it through 90 degrees (a quarter turn) and rolling it in the other direction, otherwise you will end up with an oval. The same principles apply if you want a square or a rectangle shape – simply press the pastry into roughly the right shape before rolling. Remember, if you are rolling a rectangle, you will need to roll the pastry a few more times in one direction to keep the shape from turning into a square.

If you are lining small or individual tins, then cut the pastry into 6 pieces (or however many pieces the recipe calls for) and roll each piece into a ball to begin with, then roll out each one into a circle. I find this method far easier and much less wasteful than rolling out a sheet and cutting it into circles, then having to re-roll the trimmings to fill all the tins.

Sometimes cracks will inevitably appear and it pays to patch and push them together as you go along, rather than wait until you are left with a gaping hole that will be harder to deal with. If necessary, stick bits together using a dab of cold water to firmly seal any joins. Whilst cracks are annoying, it's worth noting that the pastry that is hardest to work with often seems to be the crispest, crumbliest and most delicious to eat, so take heart from what might seem like a failure at the time!

The thickness of the pastry is important and the ideal is to roll as thinly as you can – about 3mm should be your goal. Think of the pastry as a tasty container – it's the filling that should shine through and not be overshadowed by a thick and quite possibly stodgy pastry. A 3mm thickness of pastry is typical for most of the recipes in this book, but a few specific recipes do call for a slightly thicker rolled pastry – about 4mm or 5mm – such as the Smoked Gammon and Minted Pea Pies (see page 32), Roast Beef, Sweet Potato and Horseradish Pie with Cheese Crumble Topping (see page 38), Borlotti Bean, Squash, Red Pepper and Chard Pie with Goat's Cheese (see page 80), Traditional Pork Pie (see page 34), Raised Game Pie (see page 100) and Cornish Pasties (see page 127). These particular pies need a more sturdy crust to encase a robust filling.

Chilling and Resting the Pastry

When I first learnt to cook at school (in the days when we all still did home economics!) we were always told that cold hands are best for pastry making. Whilst this is probably true, and hot sweaty hands are definitely a no no, resting the pastry in the fridge after making it is definitely more important.

When you incorporate fat into flour, you will be developing the gluten – a protein molecule – in the flour. The more you work the flour, the more elastic and stretchy the dough will become. This is obviously a desirable thing when making bread and it's why we use high gluten or strong bread flour, but with pastry, overworking with give you a tough and chewy crust. Chilling and resting allows the gluten time to relax before baking, which helps to minimise this problem. Therefore, standard plain flour is used for pastry making, although there is one pastry recipe in this book that does use strong flour and that is the Cornish Pasties recipe (see page 127) – this is the traditional way with this particular recipe, because the pastry needs to be tough and robust to keep the filling inside during a relatively long bake. A light crumbly short pastry would just not be up to the job with these pasties.

Purists tend to say that the best pastry needs to be relaxed and chilled both before and after rolling. I have to say my patience normally gets the better of me once I've rolled the pastry out, and I rarely chill it again once it's in the tin. The exception is if I'm making pastry on a very hot day and the fat has started to melt during rolling and shaping. Or, when I am making lots of little tarts, where the shrinkage factor would be very noticeable, not to mention annoying, when you can get hardly any filling in.

Trimming and Finishing Pastry Edges

You will inevitably need to trim up your pastry so it fits neatly in the tin, and in the case of puff pastry, straight and neat edges will allow for a better rise (or 'puff') in the oven during baking, so a small sharp knife is the ideal tool to use.

With blind-baked pastry tart cases (see page 10), some chefs like to bake them first then trim after, and whilst this can create a lovely neat finish, personally I find it a bit fiddly as it can create cracks if the pastry is particularly brittle, so this is not the way I recommend doing it. My way is to line the tin, making sure the pastry is really well pressed into the base and up the sides of the tin, with the excess hanging over the top edges. I then take the rolling pin and give it a swift roll across the top of the tin, neatly trimming off the excess pastry. Finally, I use my thumb and forefinger to pinch around and squeeze the pastry just a little higher than the top of the tin (a couple of millimetres or so) – this will allow for the inevitable bit of shrinkage as it bakes and creates a nice neat finish.

When making a double crust pie, or when sealing the edges of an individual pie or pasty, it's nice to crimp the edges together in wavy lines. Whilst not essential by any means (and as long as you have sealed the two edges together firmly, a straight finish is perfectly adequate), crimping the edges does add a nice finishing touch.

Glazing and Decorating Pastry

For any recipe where pastry is placed on top of the pie rather than just underneath it, it is a good idea to glaze it so it bakes to a lovely, shiny golden brown colour. The traditional way is to lightly brush the pastry with beaten egg. This is no doubt the best way for a lovely finish, but I find it can sometimes be a touch wasteful – even a sharing-size pie only seems to use about half an egg to glaze. So, for lots of pies, I tend to glaze with a half and half mixture of milk whisked with oil (olive or vegetable oil are both ideal). It gives a nice glaze, not quite so shiny as egg, but good all the same. I do sometimes use an egg glaze though, particularly for a 'special' pie – one that has taken plenty of time and love to prepare – or when I'm baking lots of pies, so I don't waste the egg. Another good glaze is lightly beaten plain egg white, which freezes brilliantly, so if I'm making a recipe that uses lots of egg yolks, I often freeze the whites in ice cube trays so I can pop one out and defrost it to use for a pie glaze.

I have to say I don't particularly go in for lots of cut pastry decorations on the tops of my pies – leaves, flowers, chickens or whatever – it's just not really my style (and my kids would be deprived of their jam tart making!). What I do like to do though, for some savoury pies, is to sprinkle over a few flakes of sea salt, or perhaps some cumin seeds, dried herbs or a pinch of smoked paprika, and for some sweet pies, a sprinkling of caster sugar is ideal – just a small easy finishing touch that will remind people that what they are eating is most definitely and deliciously homemade.

Blind-baking

Blind-baking or baking blind simply means baking a pastry case empty. The pastry case is lined with non-stick baking paper and the base is weighed down as it cooks by filling the case with ceramic baking beans, dried beans or dried rice. I have a box of dried chickpeas that are used solely for this purpose and they have been in and out of the oven hundreds of times and are still going strong.

Sometimes a recipe states you should prick the base of the case before blind-baking. I have to say I have tried it both ways many times and have concluded that providing the case is well weighted with beans, it makes little difference to the end result. However, it is something my kids enjoy doing, so if they are 'helping' me, I often let them do a bit of fork stabbing. The exception to the rule in this book is the Egg Custard Tarts recipe (see page 137), where I have forgone the lining of each muffin hole with paper and beans in favour of a good prick all over with a fork.

How to Make a Deep or Shallow 25cm Blind-baked Shortcrust Pastry Tart Case

These instructions are for blind-baking a deep or shallow 25cm shortcrust pastry tart case until it is fully cooked, which I use in a good number of recipes throughout this book.

For this, you'll need a deep or shallow 25cm plain or fluted loose-based tart tin.

Preheat the oven to 200°C/180°C fan/gas 6. It's also a good idea to place a heavy baking sheet on a shelf in the oven to heat up – that way the base of the pastry gets an instant burst of bottom heat to start the cooking process off.

Once you have lined the tin with shortcrust pastry, line the pastry case with non-stick baking paper and then fill it with baking beans, spreading them out evenly. Slide the tin onto the hot baking sheet in the oven and bake for 20 minutes. Remove the paper and beans, then bake for a further 5 minutes to cook the pastry through completely. Remove from the oven and use as required in any recipe that requires a deep or shallow 25cm blind-baked shortcrust pastry tart case.

Gluten-free Pastry

So many people these days suffer from gluten intolerance or food allergies that it feels very important to include a couple of gluten-free recipes in this book. They are not as fail-safe as regular wheat flour pastry and they are softer and harder to work with. However, they do work well, which is brilliant news if you can't eat gluten but still want to eat pie. One thing to note is that I find these pastries to be most successful when they are blind-baked before filling, so this really makes them only suitable for open tarts and quiches rather than for traditional double-crust pies. They just don't seem to be sturdy enough to support and encase a filling when cooked from raw.

Gluten-free Shortcrust Pastry

Makes about 330g | Takes 10 minutes to make (plus chilling)

85g gluten-free plain white flour blend (such as Doves Farm)
85g cornflour
a pinch of fine salt
85g cold butter, cut into small cubes
1 egg
1 tbsp ice-cold water

Make this pastry either by hand or in a food processor, in the same way that you would make regular shortcrust pastry, adding the egg and water once the flours, salt and butter have been combined to make coarse crumbs. Wrap, then chill the pastry really well after making (for at least 1 hour in the fridge) to firm it up before using.

Instead of rolling out the pastry on a flour-dusted work surface, roll it out between 2 sheets of cling film using a gentle even pressure, as this pastry is quite soft. Line a tart tin with the pastry, using the rolling pin to support the pastry as you transfer it to the tin, trim the edges, then re-chill it in the fridge for 30 minutes. Once chilled, line with non-stick baking paper and baking beans (see page 10) and blind-bake

in a preheated oven at 200°C/180°C fan/gas 6 for 20 minutes. Remove the paper and beans, then bake for a further 5 minutes or until completely cooked through. Remove from the oven and leave to cool completely before using in a suitable recipe of your choice.

You can also make a sweet version of this recipe by stirring 25g icing sugar through the combined (rubbed-in) flour and butter crumbs, before you add the egg and water.

Gluten-free Almond and Polenta Sweet Pastry

A delicate but rich gluten-free pastry that might be slightly trickier to ease from the tin, this is a great one to use as a base for sweet tarts. With this sort of pastry, I would definitely recommend letting the cooked tart cool completely in the tin before trying to remove it. Once the filling is cold it will be sturdier and will help to support the rather fragile pastry.

Makes about 405g | Takes 10 minutes to make (plus freezing and chilling)

125g ground almonds
125g fine polenta
2 tbsp caster sugar
100g cold butter, cut into small cubes
1–2 tbsp ice-cold water

You can make this pastry by hand or in a food processor, using the same method as for the Gluten-free Shortcrust Pastry (see pages 11–12). Again, this pastry is quite soft, so shape it into a log wrapped in cling film and freeze for 30 minutes, then slice it into 4mm-thick rounds. Arrange the rounds of pastry in the tin, as closely packed together as possible, then press the joins together using your hands. Smooth with the back of a spoon and chill in the fridge for a further 30 minutes or so to firm up the pastry once more.

Blind-bake following the instructions for the Gluten-free Shortcrust Pastry (see pages 11–12), but initially bake for 15 minutes only (at 200°C/180°C fan/gas 6). Remove from the oven, then remove the paper and beans, carefully pressing down any pastry that has become a little stuck to the paper as it can be slightly sticky (the back of a metal spoon is handy here). Bake for a further 10 minutes or until completely cooked through. Due to the high nut content, the top edges may start to catch and colour too much. If this happens, press strips of foil over the edges to protect them and prevent burning (this is a bit tricky to do but it's worth it). Remove from the oven and leave to cool completely before using in a suitable recipe of your choice.

Using up Leftover Pastry and Pastry Trimmings

With the best will in the world there will always be a little wastage as you trim up the pastry to fit your tin or dish. Jam tarts are a favourite way of using up trimmings in my house. Don't let your imagination stop there though. Another favourite is a lightly spread layer of Marmite over a rough square of pastry (shortcrust, puff or rough puff are all suitable), followed by a sprinkle of grated Cheddar cheese. Roll the whole lot up like a sausage, then cut into slices and place on a baking sheet (cut-side up). Bake in a preheated oven at 200°C/180°C fan/gas 6 for around 12–15 minutes or until cooked and golden, and you will have a very tasty tray of cheesy whirls. Alternatively, do the grown-up thing and spread the pastry with a little black olive and anchovy tapenade before rolling, slicing and baking.

The Importance of Cooling Fillings

Pastry performs best, that is it cooks to crisp and crumbly or golden and flaky (depending on whether you are using shortcrust, rough puff or true puff pastry), when it stays as cold as possible before it goes in the oven. Pastry does not benefit from sitting around sweating at room temperature and if it comes into contact with hot fillings, then the fat within it will start to melt instantly causing your pastry to become soft, collapsing and unworkable. Therefore, it's really important that all fillings are completely cold before they come into contact with raw pastry. However, once a pastry tart case has been blind-baked (see page 10), then it is fine if the filling is on the warm side of room temperature when it is added to the pastry case. One exception to this is with the Caramelised Red Onion, Cream and Stilton Quiche recipe (see page 76), because the onions are so scorching hot, they need a generous cooling period before they come into contact with the egg custard, otherwise they will begin to cook it instantly on contact.

Notes on Ingredients

Eggs

Throughout the book, I have used large eggs. However, the pie recipes throughout this book are pretty forgiving, so if you use medium eggs it won't really critically alter how a recipe works.

Butter

In many recipes I specify unsalted butter and the reason for this is simple – the salt in salted butter means it has a tendency to burn more easily. So, whenever a recipe calls for frying (gently or otherwise), I always suggest using unsalted butter.

For the pastry recipes, or for when butter is added more as a flavouring, in mashed potato for example, the choice of butter is yours to make.

A Note About Timings

Throughout the book, the same system of working out the total preparation (to make) and cooking (to cook) timings (given towards the top of each recipe) has been applied to keep all the recipes consistent. When making the recipes, any precooking is included in the total/overall cooking time given and not in the preparation time. The preparation time (or 'to make' time) includes the time spent, for example, chopping, stirring, rolling out pastry, lining tins, assembling a pie, and so on. The cooking time (or 'to cook' time) refers to the time when heat of any sort (hob and/or oven heat) is applied to the ingredients (for example, when frying, steaming, boiling, baking, etc). In the vast majority of cases, when using the basic pastry recipes from this chapter in the pie recipes throughout the book, the time taken to prepare and chill (and blind-bake, where applicable) these pastries is not included in the overall preparation (and cooking) times given in the pie recipes.

Oven Temperatures

All the recipes in this book have been tested in an electric fan oven, but temperatures for conventional (non-fan) electric ovens and gas ovens are also given.

Storing and Freezing Pies

Many pies freeze brilliantly, and what could be nicer than baking two pies and tucking one away in the freezer for a day when cooking is not top of your agenda? Particularly with what I call the 'traditional' meat pies – chicken, beef, venison – basically the ones where you braise or stew the meat over a long period of time, it makes perfect sense to me to batch cook both the filling and the pastry and assemble the dish to the point of baking. If you know you are planning to freeze a whole pie, I suggest freezing it assembled but with the pastry uncooked (providing your pastry wasn't frozen to begin with), to get the best results. If you are using defrosted pastry, then you should always bake the pie before it becomes safe to freeze it again. It is also possible to freeze leftovers of cooked pies. In all cases, I recommend freezing pies for up to 3 months, as the flavours will start to deteriorate over a longer period of time.

Some pies simply don't freeze brilliantly and below is a list of those I wouldn't recommend freezing. The reasons are varied, but in most cases it is simply that the main ingredients don't defrost to a pleasing texture. So although you could freeze them they would be far from their best on defrosting – these include all the mashed potato-topped pies and those with a large proportion of carrot, celery or broccoli, and I learnt to my peril that sardines never ever benefit from freezing! So, don't try to freeze the pies on these pages: pages 18, 20, 21 (filling fine, but not topping), 25, 28 (filling fine, but not topping), 31 (filling fine, but not topping); 46 (filling fine, but not topping); 49, 51, 54, 57, 59, 64, 66, 67, 69, 74, 79, 82, 85, 88, 104, 105, 108, 110, 113, 114, 122, 133, 135, 136, 137, 140, 141, 143, 144, 146, 149, 157.

Wrapping Pies

Wrapping food well is essential when freezing and I always tend to double or even triple wrap food, including pies, to make sure there is no chance of 'freezer burn' (when food gets a little frostbitten). With cooked or uncooked pastry pies, including cooked chilled sweet pies (such as Key Lime Pie, see page 145), I find a layer of greaseproof paper wrapped around the pie first is good as it won't stick to the pastry (or filling), followed by a layer of foil. Finally, I seal the lot inside a large labelled freezer bag. Individual portions of pies also freeze well in airtight boxes.

Freezing Raw Pastry

Uncooked pastry (including shortcrust, sweet shortcrust, puff, rough puff and filo) freezes superbly, so if I am making my own pastry and there is a little room in my freezer, I generally make a double batch and freeze half to make an easy pie another day. Wrap the pastry well in cling film, then seal it in a freezer bag and label. Freeze for up to 3 months, then defrost in the fridge overnight or for a couple of hours or so at a cool room temperature.

Defrosting Pies

When defrosting pies, it's best to leave them in the fridge overnight so they can defrost gently and evenly. If you don't have time to do that, you can leave the pie at a cool room temperature for a few hours, but do check that it has defrosted completely in the middle before you start to cook or reheat it. Defrost cooked chilled sweet pies thoroughly in the fridge overnight before serving.

Cooking and Reheating Defrosted Pies

If you are defrosting an assembled but uncooked pie, once it has completely defrosted, simply follow the cooking instructions given in the recipe. Do bear in mind though that if the pie is still very cold throughout, it may take an extra 5 minutes or so than the cooking time given in the recipe.

If you are simply reheating a defrosted cooked pie, once it has completely defrosted, reheat it in the oven at the original temperature it was cooked at until piping hot throughout. For a large pie (that makes several portions), this should be about 20 minutes. For smaller individual pies including pasties, tartlets and so on, the reheating time will be less, about 10–15 minutes. However, it's tricky to be precise with timings here, so the best way to check if the reheated pie is piping hot throughout is to pierce right into the centre with a metal skewer and hold it there for a generous 10 seconds or so. Remove it and immediately touch it gently to your bottom lip. If you can't hold it there beyond a second or two then the pie is hot enough to eat safely. If you are reheating a cooked pie, you may need to cover it loosely with foil partway through reheating if it is showing signs of becoming too brown.

FAMILY FAVOURITES

A generous and steaming pie placed in the centre of the family dinner table is a thing of great beauty, and something that will bring the cook a glow of heady satisfaction. Somehow the world feels better when you are presented with a pie and there is no better culinary gift you can offer to your nearest and dearest. In this chapter, you will find family-size pies from which to dig out a great spoonful or cut a generous slice, plus some individual pies to enjoy too. These are the pies your family will be begging you to make for them time and time again.

Spanakopita (Greek Feta and Spinach Pie)

This classic Greek pie is packed full of spinach and salty sharp feta, and the dill, spring onions and nutmeg are very traditional flavourings. You do need to dry the spinach very thoroughly before you pack it into the pie – a salad spinner is ideal – otherwise it gets a little soggy on cooking.

Serves 6 | Takes 25 minutes to make (plus cooling), 1 hour to cook

600g fresh spinach
1 bunch spring onions, chopped
bunch of fresh dill, chopped
200g feta, crumbled
5 tbsp olive oil
$\frac{1}{2}$ a nutmeg, freshly grated
1 pack (250g) filo pastry (about 10 sheets)
salt and freshly ground black pepper
sea salt flakes, for sprinkling

Preheat the oven to 200°C/180°C fan/gas 6. Grease a 23cm springform cake tin and line the base with non-stick baking paper. Set aside.

Wash the spinach thoroughly and squeeze dry. Spin dry in a salad spinner if you have one, or pat as dry as possible between 2 clean tea towels. It's important to get the spinach as dry as you can so that the pie is not overly wet on cooking. Tip the spinach into a large mixing bowl and mix through the spring onions, dill, feta and a couple of tablespoons of the oil. Grate in the nutmeg and season well with salt and freshly ground black pepper. Set aside.

Unroll a sheet of filo pastry onto the work surface, then cover the rest with a clean damp tea towel to keep it supple. Brush the filo sheet with a little oil, then drape it into the prepared tin, tucking well into the corners and hanging the excess over the side. Unroll another sheet of pastry and repeat. Continue in the same way spreading the sheets around the tin so the overlap hangs evenly all around the edge, until you've used approximately half of the pack of filo, reserving the remainder for the top of the pie.

Pack the spinach and feta mixture into the filo-lined tin, pressing down firmly to compact it as much as possible. Fold the overhanging pastry over the filling around the edges. Brush another sheet of filo with a little oil, then lay it over the top of the filling (and pastry edges), scrunching it up as you lay it down to create a 'wave' in the surface. Repeat this with the remaining filo sheets, brushing and scrunching each one, making sure the filling is covered completely in filo 'waves' and pressing down firmly on the edges to seal. Drizzle over the last little bit of oil and sprinkle with a few sea salt flakes and a grind of black pepper.

Bake in the oven for about 1 hour or until the pastry is crisp and golden, covering the top with a loose tent of foil if it is getting a little too dark towards the end of cooking. Remove from the oven and leave to cool in the tin for 20 minutes. Release the springform and then, using 2 fish slices, carefully slide the pie onto a serving plate or wooden board.

This pie is best served warm rather than oven hot. It's great served alongside a selection of Mediterranean-inspired salads, such as roast peppers marinated in garlic and balsamic vinegar, sweet ripe tomatoes sliced and drizzled with extra virgin olive oil, and diced cucumber dressed with herbs and black olives.

Potato, Cheese and Green Bean Pie

'Cheese pie' was a dish Dad used to make often and it was delicious, a real favourite. Mash, rich with cheese and a little garlic, was studded with bite-size pieces of green beans, topped with yet more cheese and grilled until golden and bubbling. This is still the sort of food I turn to for automatic comfort if I'm feeling under the weather. It is soothing, filling and just a little bit bland (but in a good way!) and I always, always eat it with a big dollop of ketchup.

Serves 4 | Takes 20 minutes to make, 30 minutes to cook

1.8–2kg floury potatoes, peeled and cut into equal-size chunks
200g green beans, cut into bite-size pieces
50g butter
200g mature Cheddar cheese, grated
a splash of milk
1 clove garlic, crushed
salt and freshly ground black pepper

Put the potatoes into a large saucepan and cover with cold water. Shake in a little salt and bring to the boil, then cook until they are tender, around 15–20 minutes, depending on the size you cut them.

Whilst the potatoes are cooking, boil or steam the green beans in a separate saucepan until they are just tender, around 4–5 minutes. Drain and set aside.

Preheat the grill to high.

Drain the potatoes well and leave to dry in the colander for a minute or so – watery, wet mash is really unpleasant and difficult to get smooth. Return the potatoes to the pan and mash well, making sure you get all the lumps out, particularly the ones lurking around the edges. Set the pan over a really low heat and add the butter. Using a large metal spoon, stir and beat the mashed potato until the butter has melted. Add most of the cheese, reserving a handful for the top, and beat again until it has melted. At this point, add a splash of milk to loosen the texture a little – just a tablespoon or two should do it. Beat through the crushed garlic and season well with salt and freshly ground black pepper.

Stir through the cooked beans and then spoon into a heatproof dish, levelling the surface as you go. Scatter over the remaining cheese. Place the pie under the hot grill for a few minutes or until the cheese is golden and bubbling. Serve immediately whilst piping hot. As kids we just used to eat this on its own, with the obligatory ketchup. Now I make it for my kids and they prefer it with baked beans.

A few variations
• Add a handful of cooked peas and a little chopped fresh basil in place of the green beans.
• Fry some bacon until crisp and snip into the mash and cheese.
• Replace half of the potato with cooked sweet potatoes or parsnips for a sweeter mash.
• Gently sweat a finely chopped onion in butter or olive oil until soft and melting, then stir through with the green beans.
• For a more 'adult' version use a creamy blue cheese such as Stilton, in place of the Cheddar.

Creamed Spinach and Goat's Cheese Tart

Made from blocks of frozen (defrosted) chopped spinach leaves, this speedy tart is a pretty handy recipe to have up your sleeve. The fact that you don't need to wash frozen spinach thoroughly like the fresh stuff is one great bonus. The other is that it's much more compact as effectively it's already wilted down. Have you ever wilted a massive bag of fresh spinach and it ends up barely enough for one person? With the frozen stuff you lessen the tricky quantity calculation.

Serves 3–4 (good for a supper for 2 with a few leftovers for lunch the next day) | Takes 20 minutes to make, 30 minutes to cook

500g frozen spinach 'bricks', defrosted
200g crème fraîche
2 eggs
25g fresh Parmesan cheese, finely grated
1 clove garlic, crushed
$\frac{1}{4}$–$\frac{1}{2}$ nutmeg, freshly grated, or to taste
plain flour, for dusting
$\frac{1}{2}$ pack (250g) ready-made puff pastry
75g soft rindless goat's cheese, crumbled
salt and freshly ground black pepper

Preheat the oven to 220°C/200°C fan/gas 7.

Put the blocks of defrosted spinach into a sieve and place the sieve over a bowl. Using a wooden spoon, or better still your hands, squeeze out as much juice as you possibly can – it will be quite a lot, so just keep on squeezing until the spinach is really quite dry.

Measure the crème fraîche into a mixing bowl, crack in the eggs and beat together. Stir through the Parmesan, garlic, nutmeg and a generous grind of salt and black pepper. Add the squeezed spinach and mix until it's really evenly combined. Set aside.

On a lightly floured work surface, roll out the pastry to a thickness of about 3mm – the shape doesn't really matter too much, just aim for a large square or rectangle that best fits your baking sheet. Use a sharp knife to trim the edges – neat straight edges with puff pastry are always better as they allow maximum 'puff' to be achieved on baking. Lay the sheet of pastry on a baking sheet and, using the tip of a sharp knife, score a shallow line about 1cm in from the edge all the way around the edge of the pastry to create a border – this will help the pastry to puff up at the edges.

Spoon the spinach filling onto the pastry, spreading it evenly but keeping it well within the border, then sprinkle over the goat's cheese.

Bake in the oven for around 25–30 minutes or until the pastry is crisp and golden. Serve hot or warm. A salad in contrasting colours – perhaps sliced tomatoes and cold cooked beetroot seasoned with olive oil and balsamic vinegar – is all you need alongside.

Trout and Broccoli Pie

I like to use fresh trout in this fish pie as I love the slightly earthy taste and, as a bonus, it's often a little cheaper than salmon. But do use salmon if you prefer it. When making any sort of mashed potato topping, choose a floury spud, such as Desiree, Maris Piper or King Edward, for the fluffiest mash. Waxy salad-type potatoes, such as Charlotte, don't mash to a pleasant texture. I like to serve this with carrots, jumping at any opportunity to get a few extra veg into my kids…

Serves 4 | Takes 20 minutes to make, 50 minutes to cook

For the filling
600g skinless fresh trout fillets
500ml milk
2 bay leaves
1 head of broccoli (about 300g), split into florets
50g butter
40g plain flour
bunch of fresh basil, leaves and soft stalks roughly chopped
salt and freshly ground black pepper

For the potato topping
1.2kg floury potatoes, peeled and cut into equal-size chunks
50g butter, plus a little extra to dot on the top
50–75ml milk

Preheat the oven to 200°C/180°C fan/gas 6.

For the filling, arrange the fish fillets in a single layer in a baking dish (preferably the one you plan to cook the pie in to save on washing up), cutting the fish to fit if necessary. Pour over the milk, tuck in the bay leaves and season with a little salt and freshly ground black pepper. Cover with a tight-fitting layer of foil and bake in the oven for about 15 minutes, perhaps a little more or less, depending on the thickness of the fish, until the fish is just cooked and flakes easily.

Whilst the fish is in the oven, make the potato topping. Put the potatoes into a large saucepan and cover with cold water. Shake in a little salt and bring to the boil, then cook until they are tender, around 15–20 minutes, depending on the size you cut them. Drain well and mash thoroughly to get all the lumps out. Set the pan over a really low heat and then add the butter, beating until smooth. Add just enough milk, beating well to create a smooth creamy mash and season well with salt and black pepper. Set aside.

In the meantime, boil or steam the broccoli until just tender, around 4–5 minutes. Drain and set aside. When the fish is cooked, remove from the oven and gently lift it onto a plate with a fish slice, draining as much milk as you can

back into the dish. Set the fish aside whilst you make the sauce. Remove and discard the bay leaves.

Melt the butter in a saucepan and stir through the flour to form a smooth paste or roux. Cook for a minute before gradually whisking in the warm milk. Whisk well over a medium heat until smooth and thickened, then simmer steadily for about 5 minutes to cook the flour. Remove from the heat and stir through the basil, then season to taste with a little extra salt and black pepper.

Assemble the pie by flaking the fish into the baking dish, keeping the pieces quite chunky. Scatter over the broccoli florets, then pour over the sauce. Spoon the mash over the top and use a fork to spread it evenly and fluff up the surface, making sure the filling is covered completely. Finally, dot the top with a little extra butter.

Bake in the oven for 20–25 minutes or until bubbling and hot throughout. Serve hot with a dish of extra cooked veggies on the side – carrots, peas and green beans are all lovely and kid-friendly. Ketchup is optional – I always do!

Tuna and Sweetcorn Pie with Sweet Potato Top

This really family-friendly and budget-conscious dish is the perfect thing for a satisfying midweek meal. As the name suggests, sweet potatoes make for a sweet mash, which seems very popular with kids. Sweet potatoes are a little wetter in texture than regular potatoes, so you may not need to add any milk at all to get a lovely consistency.

Serves 4–6 | Takes 20 minutes to make, 50 minutes to cook

For the filling
1 tbsp olive oil
25g unsalted butter
1 onion, finely chopped
50g plain flour
600ml milk
2 x 198g cans sweetcorn
    kernels, drained
couple of handfuls of frozen
    peas or frozen soya beans
small bunch of fresh flat-leaf
    parsley, chopped
2 x 200g cans tuna, drained
salt and freshly ground black
    pepper

For the sweet potato topping
1.2kg sweet potatoes, peeled
    and cut into equal-size
    chunks
50g butter
a splash of milk
75g mature Cheddar cheese,
    grated

For the filling, put the oil and butter into a heavy-based saucepan and set over a medium-low heat. Once the butter is melted, stir through the onion and cook, uncovered, for around 20 minutes or until soft and lightly caramelised, stirring occasionally.

Sprinkle in the flour, stirring well to mix it into the buttery juices. Gradually pour in the milk, stirring continuously to prevent any lumps forming as the sauce thickens. Bring gently to the boil and then simmer steadily for about 5 minutes to cook the flour. Remove from the heat and stir through the sweetcorn kernels, peas and parsley, then season to taste with salt and freshly ground black pepper. Gently fold through the tuna, trying not to break it up too much, then transfer the mixture to a large baking dish.

Whilst the filling mixture is cooking, make the sweet potato topping. Put the potatoes into a large saucepan and cover with boiling water. Shake over a little salt and bring to the boil, then cook for around 15–20 minutes or until they are tender. Drain well, return the sweet potatoes to the pan and allow the steam to evaporate off for a few minutes, then mash them well until really smooth. Set the pan over a really low heat, add the butter and a splash of milk to loosen the mash, if necessary,

beating until smooth, then season to taste with salt and black pepper.

Meanwhile, preheat the oven to 200°C/180°C fan/gas 6.

Spoon the mashed sweet potato over the tuna filling and level out with a fork, making sure the filling is covered completely. Sprinkle over the cheese.

Bake in the oven for around 25 minutes or until bubbling hot and crisp on top. Serve hot with a generous seasonal salad.

Salmon en Croutes with Beetroot, Capers and Parsley

Whilst salmon en croute is normally made as one big impressive-looking pie, I prefer to make mine as individual 'mini croutes'. The main reason, I think, is that everyone gets equal portions of crispy buttery pastry. If you disagree, then feel free to make one big one, using the same quantity of ingredients, but you will need to up the cooking time by 10 minutes or so, perhaps a little more, to ensure the fish is cooked through. The beetroot gives an earthy sweetness to the dish, not to mention a rather glorious colour.

Makes 4 individual croutes | Takes 25 minutes to make, 25 minutes to cook

250g pack cooked beetroot (not in vinegar), finely chopped
4 tsp capers, roughly chopped
4 tsp crème fraîche
small bunch of fresh flat-leaf parsley, chopped
plain flour, for dusting
1 pack (500g) ready-made puff pastry
500g skinless salmon loin, cut into 4 equal-size pieces (or buy 4 skinless fillets, about 125g each)
salt and freshly ground black pepper
1 egg, lightly beaten, to glaze
sea salt flakes, for sprinkling

Preheat the oven to 220°C/200°C fan/gas 7.

In a small bowl, mix together the beetroot, capers, crème fraîche and parsley. Season well with salt and freshly ground black pepper and set to one side.

On a lightly floured work surface, cut the pastry into 4 equal-size squares. Roll out each square to a thickness of about 3mm, aiming for a shape that is a little over twice the size of a piece of fish.

Spoon a quarter of the beetroot mixture down the centre of one piece of pastry, keeping it roughly to the same shape as a piece of fish. Lay a piece of fish over the beetroot mixture, pressing down lightly so the beetroot mixture and fish fit snugly together. Brush a little beaten egg onto the pastry edges and fold one side and then the other over the fish, enclosing it completely. Trim the pastry ends so they are about 1cm bigger than the fish, pressing together firmly to seal. Brush a little more beaten egg over each end, then fold them up on top, pressing firmly to stick them together. Carefully flip the parcel over so all the stuck edges are now on the bottom and place on a baking sheet. Repeat with the remaining pieces of pastry, beetroot mixture and pieces of fish.

Brush a little beaten egg all over the parcels and sprinkle each one with a few sea salt flakes. Bake in the oven for about 25 minutes or until the pastry is crisp and golden. Serve hot. Buttered asparagus or green beans and perhaps a few new potatoes are the perfect accompaniments for these pies.

Chicken and Mushroom Pot Pie

Quite simply a classic among pies, this is certainly one of my favourites and one I remember Mum often making for us when we were growing up. I always make this with cooked chicken, usually leftovers from a roast bird, but you can always start from scratch. In that case, I suggest using diced skinless boneless thigh meat as it has far more flavour than breast. Add it to the sauce as it's simmering, allowing it to cook through for 10 minutes before adding to the pie dish and cooling.

Serves 4 | Takes 20 minutes to make (plus cooling), 55 minutes to cook

50g unsalted butter
1 onion, chopped
250g chestnut mushrooms, thickly sliced
2 cloves garlic, crushed
couple of sprigs of fresh lemon thyme
50g plain flour
600ml milk
400g cold cooked chicken, shredded (leftover roast meat is ideal)
plain flour, for dusting
1/2 pack (250g) ready-made puff pastry
salt and freshly ground black pepper
a little beaten egg or a mixture of milk and vegetable oil, to glaze
sea salt flakes, for sprinkling

Melt the butter in a heavy-based saucepan set over a low heat, then stir through the onion and cook for 10 minutes or until it is starting to soften. Add the mushrooms, garlic and thyme sprigs and cook gently for another 10 minutes. As they are cooking, the mushrooms will release then reabsorb their juices.

Stir through the flour thoroughly, then gradually pour in the milk, stirring constantly to prevent any lumps forming as the sauce begins to thicken. Season with salt and freshly ground black pepper, then bring gently to the boil and simmer steadily for about 5 minutes to cook the flour. Remove from the heat and set aside to cool completely. Remove and discard the thyme stalks, stir through the chicken, and then spoon into a pie dish.

Once the vegetable mixture is cold, preheat the oven to 220°C/200°C fan/gas 7.

On a lightly floured work surface, roll out the pastry to a thickness of about 3mm. Brush the rim of the pie dish with a little cold water and lay the pastry over the filling, pressing down firmly at the edges to seal. Trim the edges with a small sharp knife, then crimp them if you like. Make a cut or two in the top of the pie to allow the steam to escape, then brush the surface with a little beaten egg or a mixture of milk and oil and sprinkle over a few sea salt flakes.

Bake in the oven for around 25–30 minutes or until the pastry is puffed up and golden and the filling is bubbling hot. Serve hot. Like most rich meaty pies, I like to serve plenty of veg alongside. I also think a traditional classic like this pie really needs a bit of mashed potato to go with it.

CHICKEN

Chicken, Cavolo Nero and Cheesy Potato Pie

Cavolo nero is a deliciously dark, almost black, Italian cabbage that is not always so easy to find in the shops. However, it grows in such lovely fountain-like clumps, I'd recommend trying to grow your own if you have a little space in your garden to do so. If you can't get any, the darker outer leaves of a Savoy cabbage or spring greens are a good second best.

Serves 4–6 | Takes 20 minutes to make, 1 hour 10 minutes to cook

For the filling
2 tbsp olive oil
8 skinless, boneless chicken thighs (about 700–800g), cut into bite-size pieces
2 onions, finely chopped
200ml white wine
2 tbsp plain flour
600ml chicken stock
250g cavolo nero leaves, finely shredded (or use Savoy cabbage leaves)
a pinch of Spanish smoked paprika (optional)
salt and freshly ground black pepper

For the cheesy potato topping
1.2kg floury potatoes, peeled and cut into equal-size chunks
50g butter
50–75ml milk
75g mature Cheddar cheese, grated

For the filling, put the oil into a large, deep frying pan and set over a high heat. Once the oil is hot, add the chicken and fry for around 8–10 minutes or until it's starting to crisp up and colour a little at the edges. Resist the temptation to stir too often or you won't get the all-important caramelisation that adds so much flavour.

Reduce the heat to as low as possible and add the onions, stirring well to mix, then continue to cook gently for a further 15 minutes, stirring occasionally. Pour in the wine, increase the heat to medium-high and let the wine bubble and reduce for 5 minutes before sprinkling in the flour, stirring well to mix it into the juices. Gradually pour in the stock, stirring all the time as it thickens. Stir through the cabbage and smoked paprika, if using, season to taste with salt and freshly ground black pepper and then simmer for 5–8 minutes or until the cabbage is tender and the chicken is cooked through, stirring once or twice. Remove from the heat and transfer to a baking dish.

Whilst the chicken mixture is cooking, make the cheesy potato topping. Put the potatoes into a large saucepan and cover with cold water. Shake in a little salt and bring to the boil, then cook until they are tender, around 15–20 minutes, depending on the size you cut them. Drain well, tip the potatoes back into the pan and allow the steam to evaporate off for a few minutes. Mash well, taking care to get all the lumps that may be lurking in the corners. Set the pan over a really low heat and then add the butter, beating until smooth. Add just enough milk, beating well to create a smooth creamy mash and then season well with salt and black pepper.

Meanwhile, preheat the oven to 200°C/180°C fan/gas 6.

Spoon the mash over the chicken, and use a fork to spread it evenly, covering the filling completely. Sprinkle over the cheese.

Bake in the oven for about 30 minutes or until bubbling hot and crisp on top. Serve hot. This pie really needs nothing served alongside it as it's all contained inside!

BEEF

Steak and Ale Pies with Herby Rough Puff Pastry

A classic pie filling of slow-braised beef in a rich beery gravy. The beef benefits from really slow gentle cooking, so this is not a job to be rushed. Buy braising beef in one whole piece and cut it up yourself. That way you can be certain you are using the same cut – ready-diced beef is sometimes made up of different cuts that may have different cooking times, resulting in an unevenly cooked filling. I make this as individual pies, pub-style, in deep ceramic pie dishes (or suitable enamel mugs). If you want to make one big sharing pie, simply increase the cooking time by 10 minutes or so.

Makes 6 individual pies (easily scaled up or down to feed more or less) | Takes 20 minutes to make (plus cooling), 3 hours to cook

3 tbsp plain flour, plus extra for dusting
1kg braising beef, cut into bite-size pieces (shin, brisket and skirt are all excellent cuts to use)
2–3 tbsp olive oil
2 onions, chopped
2 large carrots, sliced or diced
500ml dark beer
350ml beef stock
1 tsp dried mixed herbs
1 batch of Herby Rough Puff Pastry (see page 8)
salt and freshly ground black pepper
a little beaten egg or a mixture of milk and vegetable oil, to glaze
sea salt flakes, for sprinkling

Sprinkle the flour into a mixing bowl and season with a little salt and freshly ground black pepper. Add the beef and toss well to coat each piece in a little flour. Heat the olive oil in a flameproof casserole set over a high heat. When the oil is smoking hot, brown the beef in batches, a handful at a time, to seal and caramelise the edges. Transfer each batch to a plate and continue until all the beef is browned, adding a splash more olive oil, if necessary.

Reduce the heat a little, then add the onions and carrots and fry for 10 minutes or so until they begin to colour a little. Return all the beef to the casserole, along with any juices, and then pour in the beer and stock. Sprinkle in the herbs and bring gently to the boil. Reduce the heat to a minimum, cover loosely with a lid (leaving a little gap), then cook very slowly until the beef is really tender, stirring from time to time. Depending on the cut of beef you use, this can take $1^1/_2$–2 hours. Remove the lid halfway through cooking to allow the sauce to thicken.

Taste to check the seasoning, adding a little more salt and black pepper, if necessary. Remove from the heat and transfer the mixture to 6 individual pie dishes (or suitable enamel mugs). Set aside to cool completely.

Once the beef mixture is cold, preheat the oven to 220°C/200°C fan/gas 7.

Lightly dust some flour over the work surface and cut the pastry into 6 equal-size pieces, gently patting each piece into roughly the shape of your pie dishes. Roll out each piece to fit the top of the pie dish, brush the rims of the dishes with a little cold water, then lay a piece of pastry over the filling in each dish, pressing down firmly at the edges to seal. Trim the edges with a small sharp knife and cut a slit in the top of each pie to let the steam out. Brush the pastry with a little beaten egg or a mixture of milk and oil and sprinkle over a few sea salt flakes.

Bake in the oven for about 30 minutes or until the pastry is crisp and golden and the filling is bubbling hot. Serve these pies hot with mashed potato (this is a must for me, but some may think that's carb-overkill) and plenty of lightly cooked vegetables.

Shepherd's Pie

Just occasionally, for it is by no means an economical cut, I roast a whole leg of lamb super slowly all day. Rubbed all over with a little cumin and smoked paprika and studded with garlic slivers and rosemary, this is a luxurious meal of meltingly tender meat. There is far too much of it for us to eat on one day and leftovers are always put to good use. Traditionally, shepherd's pie has always been made with cooked meat, and although these days it's more commonly made with lamb mince, I actually prefer it like this – and it feels very satisfying to turn a few leftovers into a whole new meal.

Serves 4 | Takes 20 minutes to make, 1 hour 35 minutes to cook

For the filling
2 tbsp olive oil
2 large onions, chopped
3 carrots, finely diced
about 250g swede (half a smallish one), peeled and finely diced
a good pinch of dried thyme
1 tbsp plain flour
500ml lamb or beef stock
a good shake of Worcestershire sauce
1 tbsp tomato purée
450g cold roast lamb, shredded into bite-size pieces
salt and freshly ground black pepper

For the potato topping
1.2kg floury potatoes, peeled and cut into equal-size chunks
50g butter
50–75ml milk

First, make the filling. Heat the oil in a large, deep frying pan or saucepan set over a medium-low heat. Stir through the onions and leave them to cook gently, uncovered, for around 30 minutes or so until really soft and lightly caramelised, stirring from time to time. Add the carrots, swede and thyme and season with salt and freshly ground black pepper, then cook gently for a further 10 minutes.

Sprinkle over the flour and stir well until evenly mixed. Gradually stir in the stock, followed by the Worcestershire sauce and tomato purée. Bring to the boil, then reduce the heat, cover and simmer for 15 minutes, stirring occasionally. Stir in the shredded lamb, then simmer, uncovered, for a further 15 minutes or until the vegetables are cooked through and the sauce is thick and rich, stirring occasionally. Taste to check the seasoning, adding a little more salt and black pepper, if necessary.

Whilst the filling is cooking, prepare the potato topping. Put the potatoes into a large saucepan and cover with cold water. Shake in a little salt and bring to the boil, then cook until they are tender, around 15–20 minutes, depending on the size you cut them. Drain well, tip the potatoes back into the pan and allow the steam to evaporate off for a few minutes. Mash thoroughly until all the lumps have gone, set the pan over a really low heat and then add the butter, beating until smooth. Add just enough milk, beating to create a smooth creamy mash, and season well with salt and black pepper.

Meanwhile, preheat the oven to 200°C/180°C fan/gas 6.

Transfer the lamb mixture to a baking dish and then spoon the mash over the top. Use a fork to level and fluff up the surface, making sure the lamb mixture is covered completely.

Bake in the oven for 20–25 minutes or until the topping is crisp and golden and the filling is starting to bubble up a little. Serve hot. This pie doesn't really need anything served alongside, except perhaps a dish of something green – lightly buttered peas or cabbage are my choice.

PORK

Quiche Lorraine

Although loved by many, the nature of the filling in this simple quiche is a little controversial. Originally from the Lorraine region of rural France, at its simplest it would have just consisted of a pastry case filled with a rich savoury egg custard and a little bacon. It almost certainly would not have included cheese, and definitely no tomato, but I like it with both, so here is my rather unauthentic but nevertheless very tasty version.

Serves 4–6 | Takes 15 minutes to make, 45 minutes to cook

200g smoked streaky bacon
150g mature Cheddar cheese, grated
1 deep 25cm blind-baked Shortcrust Pastry Tart Case (see pages 6–7)
1 large tomato, thinly sliced
100g crème fraîche
4 eggs
300ml milk
salt and freshly ground black pepper

Preheat the oven to 200°C/180°C fan/gas 6.

Fry the bacon in its own fat in a pan for around 5–8 minutes or until it is cooked and lightly crisp. Remove from the pan, drain on kitchen paper and leave to cool slightly, then snip into bite-size pieces.

Scatter about half of the cheese over the base of the pastry tart case, then add the snipped bacon. Lay over the tomato slices, spacing them evenly, then scatter over the rest of the cheese.

Whisk the crème fraîche and eggs together in a bowl until they are smooth and combined. Pour in the milk, whisking well until combined, then season with salt and freshly ground black pepper. Slowly pour into the pastry tart case.

Bake in the oven for 30–35 minutes or until the filling is just set and the top is lightly golden. Carefully remove the quiche from the tin and place it on a serving plate or wooden board. Serve hot or warm with a generous mixed salad on the side.

Cottage Pie

This was a family favourite when I was a child and if Dad was at the stove, there always seemed to be parsnips in the filling, which added a lovely sweetness. The vegetables can be diced or grated depending on how obvious you want them to be in the end dish – I know some parents find it handy to hide their presence! When you fry the mince, it's important to let it take on some colour, as this caramelisation will add lots of essential flavour. As kids we used to eat this with peas and plenty of ketchup, just as we still do today.

Serves 4 | Takes 20 minutes to make, 1¾ hours to cook

For the filling
2 tbsp olive oil
500g minced beef
1 large onion, finely chopped
2 cloves garlic, crushed
2 carrots, diced or grated
1 parsnip, diced or grated
400g can chopped tomatoes
500ml beef or vegetable stock
1 tsp dried mixed herbs
1 tsp Marmite
a shake of Worcestershire sauce
salt and freshly ground black pepper

For the potato topping
1.2kg floury potatoes, peeled and cut into equal-size chunks
50g butter
50–75ml milk
40g mature Cheddar cheese, grated (optional)

First, make the filling. Heat the oil in a deep frying pan over a medium-high heat, then add the mince and fry until it starts to take on a little colour, breaking up the meat with a wooden spoon as it cooks – this will take around 10 minutes. Resist the temptation to stir too frequently, otherwise the pan will cool down and the meat will sweat rather than fry.

Add the onion, reducing the heat a little, and continue to cook for a further 10 minutes or so until it starts to soften. Add the garlic, carrots and parsnip and fry for another minute before pouring in the tomatoes and stock. Season with the herbs, Marmite, Worcestershire sauce and a little salt and freshly ground black pepper. Bring to the boil, reduce the heat to a minimum and simmer, uncovered, for 50–60 minutes or until thick and rich, stirring occasionally. Adjust the seasoning to taste, adding a little more salt and black pepper, if necessary.

Whilst the mince mixture is simmering, prepare the potato topping. Put the potatoes into a large saucepan and cover with cold water. Shake in a little salt and bring to the boil, then cook until they are tender, around 15–20 minutes, depending on the size you cut them. Drain well, tip the potatoes back into the pan and allow the steam to evaporate off

for a few minutes. Mash thoroughly until all the lumps have gone, set the pan over a really low heat and then add the butter, beating until smooth. Add just enough milk beating to create a smooth creamy mash, and season well with salt and black pepper.

Meanwhile, preheat the oven to 200°C/180°C fan/gas 6.

Transfer the mince filling to a baking dish and then spoon the mash over the top. Use a fork to level and fluff up the surface, making sure the mince mixture is covered completely. Scatter the grated cheese over the top, if using.

Bake in the oven for 20–25 minutes or until the topping is crisp and golden and the filling is starting to bubble up a little. Alternatively, if you are short of time, crisp up the top under a preheated hot grill for around 5–8 minutes, making sure that both the filling and mash are piping hot throughout before you add them to the baking dish. Serve hot. For me it has to be peas with this, frozen are fine. I use them often and will go as far as to say that peas are one of my very favourite vegetables in the world.

Smoked Gammon and Minted Pea Pies

Begin this recipe 24 hours in advance, as the peas really do need to soak overnight. For this hearty and filling dish, I put the mushy pea element within the pie and it really is rather a success, even if I say so myself, but it's still best to serve it with the mash and gravy.

**Makes 6 individual pies |
Takes 25 minutes to make
(plus soaking and cooling),
1 hour 20 minutes to cook**

**250g dried marrowfat peas
  (such as Batchelors Bigga
  brand)
1 tsp bicarbonate of soda
1 small uncooked smoked
  gammon joint (about 750g)
2 bay leaves
1 tsp whole black
  peppercorns
1 tbsp whole cloves
50g unsalted butter
1 onion, finely chopped
generous bunch of fresh mint,
  leaves picked and finely
  chopped
plain flour, for dusting
treble batch of Shortcrust
  Pastry (see pages 6–7)
freshly ground black pepper
a little beaten egg or a
  mixture of milk and
  vegetable oil, to glaze**

The night before you want to make your pies, put the peas into a large bowl, cover generously with cold water and then stir through the bicarbonate of soda. Leave to soak overnight at room temperature – a minimum of 12 hours is necessary, but 16 won't hurt.

The next day, drain the peas and rinse well under running cold water. Place the drained peas in a saucepan and cover with cold water so that it comes about 1cm above the level of the peas. Bring to the boil and simmer steadily, uncovered, for around 40 minutes or until the peas are thick and broken down, stirring occasionally – they don't call them mushy for no reason! Towards the end of cooking, stir them frequently so they don't stick on the bottom of the pan.

Meanwhile, place the gammon joint in a separate large saucepan and cover generously with cold water, then add the bay leaves, peppercorns and cloves. Bring to a steady simmer, then half-cover with a lid and simmer for around 45 minutes for a 750g joint. Gammon takes 30 minutes per 500g to cook by boiling, so adjust your cooking time a little if your joint is a touch smaller or bigger. Once cooked, remove from the heat and remove the gammon to a plate. Reserve a little of the cooking liquor and discard the rest. Leave the gammon to cool a little before dicing it into 1cm chunks.

In the meantime, melt the butter in a frying pan set over a low heat. Stir through the onion and cook gently, uncovered, for about 30 minutes or until really soft and translucent, stirring every now and then.

Once the peas, gammon and onion are all ready, stir them together, adding a tablespoonful or two of the reserved gammon cooking liquor. Season well with freshly ground black pepper – you probably won't need to add any salt because of the gammon. Set aside to cool completely, then stir through the mint.

Once the filling is cold, preheat the oven to 200°C/180°C fan/gas 6.

On a lightly floured work surface, cut the pastry into 6 equal-size pieces, then cut about a third off each piece and set aside (these smaller bits will become the lids). Roll out the larger pieces into circles about 4mm thick – they will be the size of a generous saucer (the pastry needs to be slightly thicker here as the pies have no tins to support them so the thicker pastry is more robust). Spread out the circles over a couple of baking sheets. Using a spoon and your hands, divide the filling mixture into 6 equal portions and shape each one into a rough sphere about the size of a tennis ball, then place one in the centre of each pastry circle.

Roll out the 6 smaller pieces of pastry to circles about 4mm thick and lay each one over a sphere of filling, allowing it to drape down over the filling. Brush a little water all over the pastry edges, and then carefully bring them up to form sides, folding, crimping and pressing down firmly at the edges to seal the filling in completely. Cut a slit in the top of each pie to let the steam out and then brush all over with a little beaten egg or a mixture of milk and oil.

Bake in the oven for around 30–35 minutes or until the pastry is cooked through and golden brown. These pies are best served straight from the oven whilst piping hot. And don't forget the mash and gravy to serve alongside…

Traditional Pork Pie

With a simple filling of just two types of pork, seasoning here is key. Be generous, as with anything served cold, you will need extra seasoning for it to be flavourful. A note on the shape of tin to use to make the pork pie: as with all bottom crust pies, a metal tin is ideal here to achieve the best crust. I use a small enamel basin with a flat bottom that is 14cm in diameter and 8cm deep. A small cake tin of similar dimensions makes a good alternative too, or failing that, a small loaf tin will make a lovely rectangular pie.

Serves 6 | Takes 40 minutes to make (plus chilling, cooling and overnight chilling), 1¹/₂ hours to cook

For the filling
400g meaty rindless pork belly, cut into 1cm cubes
175g uncooked gammon (smoked or unsmoked), cut into 1cm cubes
1 tsp ground white pepper, or to taste
1 tsp ground allspice, or to taste
¹/₂ nutmeg, freshly grated
3 bay leaves, finely chopped
salt and freshly ground black pepper

1 batch of Hot Water Crust Pastry (see page 8)

For the jelly
2 leaves of gelatine
1 ham stock cube
200ml boiling water

To make the filling, simply put all the ingredients into a food processor, being rather generous with the spices and salt and freshly ground black pepper, and whizz to form a coarse paste. Transfer the paste to a bowl, press a layer of cling film down on the surface and chill in the fridge for at least 2 hours. Allowing time for the flavours to mingle like this is crucial: more time is fine, even overnight will not hurt.

Once the filling is ready, make the pastry (see page 8), then wrap, shape and chill it in the fridge for 30–45 minutes to firm up, as directed.

Preheat the oven to 180°C/160°C fan/gas 4, and place a heavy baking sheet on a shelf in the oven to heat.

Cut 2 long strips of double-thickness non-stick baking paper and use it to line your tin (see note on shape of tin to use in recipe introduction) in a cross shape, with the 4 tails hanging over the edge – this will really help you get the pie out of the tin after baking. Cut about two-thirds of the pastry into 1cm-thick discs, then place them next to each other in the tin, pressing them out and squeezing them together firmly to make a single lining of pastry that is about 5mm thick all over, with around 1cm overhanging the top of the tin. Shape the remaining pastry into a flat disc, big enough to cover the top of your pie, again making it about 5mm thick. You may have a little pastry left over, depending on the shape of the tin.

Pack the meat filling into the pastry-lined tin, pressing quite firmly so that it fills all the gaps, then top with the remaining flat pastry disc. Fold the overhanging pastry over the edges of the flat pastry disc on top, crimping all around the edges to seal. Pierce the top in the centre, twisting the knife to make a generous hole of about 5mm. Slide the pie onto the hot baking sheet in the oven and bake for about 1¹/₂ hours or until the pastry is crisp and golden brown. Remove from the oven and leave the pie to cool to room temperature in the tin.

Once the pie is cool, take a skewer and insert it into the hole in the top, piercing down through the meat and giving it a little wiggle to widen the hole.

To make the jelly, soak the gelatine sheets in cold water for 10 minutes to soften, then gently squeeze out the excess water. Crumble the stock cube into a jug and pour over the boiling water, then add the soaked gelatine, stirring until dissolved. Set aside to cool to room temperature. Slowly pour this liquid into the hole in the top of the cooled pie – a funnel will help this considerably. You may not need all of the liquid, just fill it up as much as you can. Transfer the pie to the fridge and chill overnight.

When ready to serve, use the paper tails to help lift the pie out of the tin, sliding a table knife around to ease the pie away from the edges of the tin if it is a little stuck. A pork pie is perfect picnic food, as its solid crust protects it during transit. A good chutney is the ideal accompaniment. Serve cold.

Sausage and Cannellini Bean Pie

Kids and grown-ups alike love sausages, which makes them great for family meals. My kids also love baked beans, but are inherently suspicious of any other sort of bean. Shrouding cannellini beans in a rich tomato sauce was originally my attempt to get them to try a new bean and it worked! I use ready-rolled puff pastry; it's a little more expensive than the unrolled stuff, but for a low-faff midweek pie it is convenient. If you prefer ready-made puff pastry and to roll it yourself, about half a pack (250g) should do it.

Serves 4 | Takes 20 minutes to make (plus cooling), 1¹⁄₄ hours to cook

450g chipolata sausages
2 tbsp olive oil
2 onions, chopped
2 cloves garlic, crushed
2 x 400g cans chopped tomatoes
1 tbsp tomato purée
1 tsp granulated sugar
2 x 400g cans cannellini beans, drained and rinsed
bunch of fresh basil, leaves picked and chopped
1 pack (320g) ready-rolled puff pastry (1 rectangular sheet)
salt and freshly ground black pepper
a little beaten egg or a mixture of milk and vegetable oil, to glaze

Grill or fry the sausages for about 15 minutes or until golden brown, turning occasionally, then remove from the heat and cut into bite-size chunks. Set aside.

Meanwhile, heat the olive oil in a heavy-based saucepan, then add the onions and fry over a medium-low heat for around 10 minutes or until they are starting to soften and take on just a little colour. Add the garlic and fry for a further minute before pouring in the tomatoes and about 200ml cold water. Stir through the tomato purée and sugar and season with a little salt and freshly ground black pepper. Bring to a steady simmer, then cook, uncovered, over a medium-low heat for about 30 minutes or until the sauce is thick and rich, stirring every now and then. About halfway through cooking, stir through the canned beans.

Remove from the heat and stir through the sausage chunks and basil, then adjust the seasoning to taste, adding more salt and black pepper, if needed. Transfer to a large rectangular baking dish and set aside to cool completely.

Once the filling is cold, preheat the oven to 220°C/200°C fan/gas 7.

Dampen the rim of the baking dish with a little cold water and then unroll the pastry over the filling, pressing down firmly at the edges to seal. If the pastry is slightly too small for the dish you have chosen, just roll it a touch thinner to get it to fit. Trim the pastry edges with a small sharp knife, cut a slit in the top of the pie to let the steam out and brush the surface with a little beaten egg or a mixture of milk and oil.

Bake in the oven for 25–30 minutes or until the pastry is crisp and golden. Serve hot. This pie is good served with courgettes that have been sautéed in butter and garlic.

Parmesan Polenta-topped Bolognese Pie

An Italian slant on that British classic, Cottage Pie. It's a similar dish, but there's more veg, more garlic, more herbs, a little wine and crucially, the potato topping has been replaced by a rich, buttery Parmesan polenta. Do check the packet instructions for the instant polenta – yours might need a little more or less water to rehydrate it. It's very forgiving to work with, not to mention super quick, so just adjust the liquid accordingly.

Serves 4–6 | Takes 20 minutes to make, 2$\frac{1}{4}$ hours to cook

For the filling
2 tbsp olive oil
500g minced beef
2 onions, chopped
2 peppers (any colour), deseeded and chopped
2 carrots, diced
3 cloves garlic, crushed
400g can chopped tomatoes
500ml beef stock
150ml red wine (or extra stock)
1 tbsp tomato purée
1 tsp dried oregano
salt and freshly ground black pepper

For the polenta topping
1 litre boiling water
1 tbsp vegetable bouillon powder
200g instant polenta
100g fresh Parmesan cheese, finely grated
bunch of fresh basil, leaves picked and chopped
25g butter, or a little bit more for extra richness

First, make the filling. Put the oil into a large, deep frying pan and set over a high heat. When the oil is hot, add the mince and fry for around 10 minutes or until it is nicely browned, stirring only occasionally to break the mince up. Resist the temptation to stir too often – the caramelisation of the meat is important for flavour.

Reduce the heat to a minimum, add the onions, peppers, carrots and garlic and fry for a further 5 minutes. Pour in the tomatoes, stock and wine, then stir through the tomato purée and oregano. Season with a little salt and freshly ground black pepper. Bring to the boil, then reduce the heat and simmer as gently as possible, uncovered, until the sauce is rich and thick. The longer and more slowly you cook this the better – 1$\frac{1}{2}$ hours won't be too much – it doesn't need any more attention than the very occasional stir. Once the meat sauce is cooked, transfer it to a large baking dish.

Preheat the oven to 200°C/180°C fan/gas 6.

To make the polenta topping, pour the boiling water into a large saucepan and stir through the bouillon powder. Set over a medium heat and once it's simmering again, slowly pour in the polenta, stirring all the time to prevent any lumps forming. Leave

the polenta to thicken and bubble away for a couple of minutes (the polenta might splatter a bit, so be careful), then remove from the heat.

Stir through the Parmesan (reserving a spoonful or two to scatter over the top) and basil, adding the butter to taste, and season well with salt and black pepper. Spoon the polenta mixture over the meat filling and level out with the back of a spoon, making sure the filling is covered completely. Scatter over the remaining Parmesan.

Bake in the oven for about 25 minutes or until the top is lightly golden and the filling is bubbling. Serve hot. This pie is great served on its own, or perhaps with a crunchy green salad dressed with olive oil and balsamic vinegar.

Curried Lamb Pies

My husband once 'treated' me to a 'balti pie' during a very chilly mid-winter football match. It was a pretty grim eating experience, but the concept is a great one. So, my version is a proper curry pie full of heady spices and tender meat – a million miles away from that flavourless matchday offering!

Makes 4 individual pies | Takes 25 minutes to make (plus cooling), 2 hours 25 minutes to cook

For the ground spices
2 tbsp coriander seeds
1 tbsp cumin seeds
2 tsp mustard seeds
1 tsp whole black peppercorns
2–3 dried red chillies, to taste
2 bay leaves

For the curry
2 large onions, roughly
  chopped
5 cloves garlic, peeled
5cm piece of fresh root ginger,
  peeled and roughly chopped
2 tbsp vegetable oil
600g boneless stewing lamb
  (such as neck or shoulder),
  diced
400g butternut squash (about
  ¹/₂ small/medium squash),
  deseeded and cut into 3cm
  cubes (peel left on)
50g dried yellow split peas
3 tomatoes, chopped
1 tbsp tomato purée
2 tsp granulated sugar
6 cardamom pods, left whole
a small bunch of fresh
  coriander, chopped

plain flour, for dusting
double batch of Shortcrust
  Pastry (see pages 6–7)
salt, to taste
a little beaten egg or a
  mixture of milk and
  vegetable oil, to glaze

To prepare the ground spices, tip the coriander, cumin and mustard seeds, along with the peppercorns, into a small frying pan and toast over a medium-high heat for just a minute or so until their aroma wafts up from the pan. Remove from the heat and tip into a spice mill, adding the dried chillies and bay leaves, and grind to a powder. If you don't have a spice mill, finely chop the dried chillies and bay leaves and grind the toasted spices as finely as you can using a pestle and mortar. Set aside.

For the curry, put the onions, garlic and ginger into a food processor and whizz together to form a smooth paste, adding 2 tablespoons of cold water to help it along. Pour the oil into a large saucepan and set over a medium-low heat until hot, then add the puréed onion mixture and cook gently for about 15 minutes or until translucent, stirring occasionally.

Add the lamb, squash and split peas and then pour in 600ml cold water. Stir through the tomatoes, tomato purée, sugar, cardamom pods and a little salt. Bring to the boil, then reduce the heat to a gentle simmer, cover and cook for 1–1¹/₂ hours or until the lamb is really tender. Stir from time to time and add a splash more water if it is getting a little dry. Towards the end of cooking, remove the lid to allow the sauce to thicken. Taste to check the seasoning and add a little more salt, if necessary. Remove from the heat, stir in the chopped coriander and then set aside to cool completely – spreading the curry out on a shallow tray will speed this up considerably. Remove and discard the cardamom pods.

Once the filling is cold, preheat the oven to 200°C/180°C fan/gas 6.

On a lightly floured work surface, cut the pastry into 2 pieces, making one piece slightly larger than the other. Cut the larger piece into 4 equal-size pieces, gently rolling each one into a ball. Roll out each ball to a thickness of about 3mm and use it to line an individual pie tin (each about 16 x 11cm), gently pressing down into the base and up the sides of the tin. Fill each pie with the curry and then brush the rims of the pastry with a little cold water. Cut the other piece of pastry into 4 equal-size pieces, then roll out each one as before to form the lids. Lay the lids over the pies, pressing down firmly to seal the edges and then trim the edges with a small sharp knife. Brush all over with a little beaten egg or a mixture of milk and oil and then cut a slit or two in the top of each pie to let the steam out.

Bake in the oven for around 35–40 minutes or until the pastry is cooked through and golden brown. Serve hot with your favourite Indian pickle and perhaps a crunchy salad drizzled with a raita-style dressing of natural yogurt, chopped fresh coriander and mint and crushed garlic.

Roast Beef, Sweet Potato and Horseradish Pie

I have a small confession to make, and I know many will disagree with me wholeheartedly, but I have never been too keen on cold roast beef. So, this recipe was simply designed to use up leftovers in a way more pleasing to me than a sandwich, and I have to say it was a triumphant success. For a more intense hot flavour, try to use grated horseradish (available in jars) rather than a creamy horseradish sauce, which can be quite mild-tasting.

Serves 4 | Takes 20 minutes to make (plus cooling), 1 hour 25 minutes to cook

For the pie
2 tbsp olive oil
2 large onions, chopped
2 sprigs of fresh rosemary, leaves picked and roughly chopped
600g sweet potatoes, peeled and cut into 2cm chunks
300ml beef stock
300g cold roast beef, cut into bite-size pieces
2–3 tbsp grated horseradish (available in jars), or horseradish sauce for a milder flavour
plain flour, for dusting
1 batch of Shortcrust Pastry (see pages 6–7)
salt and freshly ground black pepper

For the crumble topping
100g plain flour
50g butter, chilled and cut into little cubes
75g mature Cheddar cheese, grated

To make the pie, put the oil into a large frying pan and set over a medium heat. Once the oil is hot, add the onions, along with the rosemary, and fry for 15–20 minutes or until lightly caramelised, stirring from time to time. Stir through the sweet potatoes and then pour in the stock, seasoning well with salt and freshly ground black pepper. Bring to the boil, then cover with a piece of damp greaseproof paper pressed down over the sweet potatoes, tucking it under snugly at the edges – this creates a steamy lid to help cook the sweet potatoes. Simmer until soft – this will take around 15 minutes, depending on the size of the chunks.

Remove and discard the paper – the sweet potatoes should have absorbed most of the stock; if it is still quite liquid, then simmer, uncovered, for a few minutes. Remove from the heat, stir through the beef and horseradish and set aside to cool completely.

Once the filling is cold, preheat the oven to 200°C/180°C fan/gas 6.

On a lightly floured work surface, roll out the pastry to a thickness of about 4mm (the pastry needs to be slightly thicker here as the filling is robust so it needs a sturdy crust to hold it in) and use it to line a 23cm springform cake tin, bringing it about 4cm up the sides of the tin. Spoon in the filling, levelling it out as you go.

For the crumble topping, lightly rub the flour and butter together in a mixing bowl. When the mixture resembles breadcrumbs, mix through the cheese and season well with salt and black pepper. Sprinkle the crumble mixture evenly over the pie filling, but don't pat or press it down as you want to leave it light and airy.

Bake in the oven for 40–45 minutes or until the pastry is cooked through and the crumble topping is crisp and golden. Remove from the oven, leave to cool for a few minutes, then slide a knife around the inside of the tin and release the springform. Carefully transfer the pie to a serving plate or wooden board and serve hot. Green vegetables on the side are a great accompaniment for this pie, and perhaps a little extra horseradish sauce for those who like things fiery.

Sausage and Apple Lattice Pie

This is what I call a minimum fuss pie – one where there is no precooking of any filling, you just roll out your pastry, chop everything up, layer it in, cover it up and shove it in the oven. Job done. As a bit of a heat addict, I like to add a generous smear of English mustard to the base of the pie to spice things up a bit. If you are serving this to young children you will probably want to save your mustard for the side.

Serves 4–6 | Takes 25 minutes to make, 1 hour to cook

plain flour, for dusting
double batch of Shortcrust Pastry (see pages 6–7)
600g pork sausages
1 tbsp English mustard (optional)
2 eating apples, cored and cut into 5mm-thick slices
1 onion, thinly sliced
salt and freshly ground black pepper
1 tbsp milk mixed with 1 tbsp vegetable oil, to glaze
sea salt flakes, for sprinkling

Preheat the oven to 200°C/180°C fan/gas 6.

On a lightly floured work surface, cut the pastry into 2 pieces, making one piece slightly larger than the other. Roll out the larger piece to a thickness of about 3mm and big enough to fit a deep pie plate (about 23–25cm in diameter). Carefully lift the pastry into the pie plate, using the rolling pin to help you support it, pressing the pastry well into the bottom and up the sides and allowing the excess to hang over the edge.

Skin the sausages by running a sharp knife down the length of each, then peel the skin away and discard. Cut the sausagemeat into bite-size pieces.

Spread the mustard, if using, over the base of the pie, then scatter in a few pieces of sausagemeat, followed by a few slices of apple and onion, tucking everything in snugly. Season with a little salt and freshly ground black pepper. Repeat until you have used up all the ingredients. Pile the filling up high to make a big rounded pie – it shouldn't collapse if you press each layer down firmly as you build the pie.

Roll out the other piece of pastry, again to a thickness of about 3mm, and then cut it into 1cm wide strips. Brush a little cold water all around the pastry rim in the pie plate, then lay half of the strips of pastry across the filling in one direction, leaving about a 1cm gap between each strip, pressing down firmly to seal them to the pastry rim. Turn the pie through 90 degrees and repeat with the remaining strips, making a criss-cross pattern. You may need to squidge together the offcuts of pastry and re-roll to create the last few strips. (However, if you have any leftover pastry, see page 12 for ideas on how to use it.) Brush all over with the milk and oil glaze and then sprinkle over a few sea salt flakes.

Bake in the oven for about 50–60 minutes or until the filling is cooked and the pastry is crisp and golden brown. After about 50 minutes, pierce through one of the gaps in the lattice in the top of the pie with a skewer to see if the apples are tender. If not, return the pie to the oven to cook for a little longer. If the pastry is getting too dark, you may need to cover it loosely with a piece of foil.

Serve hot or warm. This is a good pie to serve with a big jug of steaming hot gravy. Add a bowl of cooked peas and perhaps some mashed potato and you will have a very hearty meal indeed.

Pork and Sweet Pepper Empanada

An empanada is a large flat pie from Spain that has a wine-enriched crust; a cross between pastry and bread dough. Empanadas usually have a sweet base of slowly cooked peppers and onions at their heart, sometimes with tuna and eggs as well. This variation has Moorish overtones with cumin and fennel-spiced pork stirred through the peppers before baking.

Serves 6–8 | Takes 25 minutes to make (plus cooling and rising), 1 hour 40 minutes to cook

For the filling
2 tbsp olive oil
400g minced pork
2 tsp coriander seeds
2 tsp cumin seeds
2 tsp fennel seeds
1 tsp Spanish smoked paprika
4 large mixed peppers, deseeded and sliced
3 large onions, sliced
3 cloves garlic, crushed
2 tbsp sherry vinegar
bunch of fresh flat-leaf parsley, chopped
salt and freshly ground black pepper
beaten egg, to glaze
sea salt flakes, for sprinkling

For the dough
1 tsp dried yeast
4 tbsp hand-hot water, plus extra for binding the dough
1 tsp caster sugar
350g strong white bread flour, plus extra for dusting
125g fine polenta
a pinch of salt
100ml white wine
25ml olive oil, plus extra for brushing
50g lard or vegetable fat, cut into small dice
1 egg, lightly beaten

To make the filling, put 1 tablespoon of the oil into a large, deep frying pan and set over a high heat. Once the oil is hot, add the mince, breaking it up with a wooden spoon. Stir through the coriander, cumin and fennel seeds and the smoked paprika and fry for around 10–15 minutes or until the meat is crisped up a little at the edges and golden – don't stir too often otherwise the meat won't brown easily. Transfer the mince mixture to a plate and set aside.

Reduce the heat to as low as possible and add the remaining oil to the pan, followed by the peppers and onions. Cook very gently, uncovered, for at least 45 minutes, or perhaps even 1 hour, until they are really soft and almost melting, stirring occasionally. Season with salt and freshly ground black pepper, add the garlic and sherry vinegar and cook for another 5 minutes. Remove from the heat, stir through the minced pork mixture and the parsley and set aside to cool completely – spreading the mixture out on a shallow tray will speed this up considerably.

Whilst the filling is simmering, make the dough. Activate the yeast by mixing it with the measured hand-hot water and caster sugar in a small bowl, stirring until dissolved, then set aside for 10 minutes – it should start gently bubbling.

In a large mixing bowl, stir together the flour and polenta with the pinch of salt. Pour in the wine and oil, then add the lard, egg and activated yeast liquid. Add enough extra warm water, mixing to bring it all together to make a soft, pliable dough. Turn the dough onto the work surface and knead for a couple of minutes, but don't overdo it, it just needs to be well mixed and look smooth – if you over-knead the dough it can become a little tough on baking. Transfer the dough to a clean oiled bowl and cover with cling film. Leave to rise until it has doubled in size – an hour or two in a warmish room should do it.

Preheat the oven to 220°C/200°C fan/gas 7.

Turn the dough onto a lightly floured work surface and cut it in half. Roll out each piece into a large square-ish shape (to a thickness of about 5mm). Lay one piece of dough on a baking sheet, then pile the cold filling on top and spread it out in an even layer, leaving a generous 2cm border all around the edge. Lay the second sheet of dough over the top, crimping and folding the edges over to completely seal in the filling. Brush with the beaten egg and scatter over a few flakes of sea salt.

Bake in the oven for around 30–35 minutes or until the crust is cooked, golden and crisp. This pie is best served at room temperature (if you can wait that long). Serve on its own or with a seasonal salad, if you like. Wrapped in its sturdy pastry case, a cooked whole empanada is also a fabulous thing to take on a picnic, ready to be sliced up and served cold.

FRUGAL PIES

Pies are a gorgeous way of using up leftovers and odds and sods from the fridge, and a lovingly-made pie will belie the frugality of the ingredients, giving you something to eat that is so much more than the sum of its meagre parts. It's amazing what you can rustle up with just half a pack of pastry, a handful of vegetables, a little cheese and a couple of eggs. Here, you will find a wealth of ideas to help you make the most of the ingredients lurking in your kitchen and create some truly tempting pies, including quiches, tarts and strudels.

Puy Lentil and Roast Butternut Squash 'Shepherd's Pies'

Puy lentils are great for adding texture to vegetarian meals as they don't collapse on cooking. In this pie, they are simmered in a rich tomato sauce and combined with roast butternut squash to make a meat-free base to a comforting shepherd's pie. I make this either as four generous individual pies (as I do here) or as one large pie. If you are making one large pie, simply assemble in a baking dish and increase the baking time in the oven to around 30 minutes.

Makes 4 generous individual pies | Takes 25 minutes to make, 1 hour to cook

For the filling
1 small butternut squash (about 700g), deseeded and cut into 2–3cm chunks (I leave the peel on for texture)
2 large onions, cut into wedges
3 tbsp olive oil
200g Puy lentils
500ml vegetable stock
400g can chopped tomatoes
1 tbsp tomato purée
2 cloves garlic, crushed
2 bay leaves
2 sprigs of fresh thyme or 1/2 tsp dried thyme
salt and freshly ground black pepper

For the potato topping
1kg floury potatoes, peeled and cut into equal-size chunks
50g butter, plus a little extra to dot on the top
50ml milk

Preheat the oven to 200°C/180°C fan/gas 6.

For the filling, put the squash and onions into a large roasting tin, drizzle over the oil, season with a little salt and freshly ground black pepper, then toss the vegetables to coat all over. Roast in the oven for around 35–40 minutes or until the vegetables are soft and a little caramelised at the edges – give them a stir about halfway through cooking. Remove from the oven.

Meanwhile, tip the lentils into a sieve and rinse well under cold running water, then drain and place in a saucepan. Pour in the stock and tomatoes, then stir through the tomato purée, garlic, bay leaves and thyme. Set over a medium heat and bring to the boil, then reduce the heat and simmer, uncovered, for around 20 minutes or until the lentils are just tender, stirring from time to time. Remove from the heat, then remove and discard the bay leaves and thyme stalks.

In the meantime, prepare the potato topping. Put the potatoes into a large saucepan and cover with cold water. Shake in a little salt and bring to the boil, then cook until they are tender, around 15–20 minutes, depending on the size you cut them. Drain well, tip the potatoes back into the pan and allow the steam to evaporate off for a few minutes. Set the pan over a really low heat and mash the potatoes well with the butter and milk, beating to make a smooth creamy mash, then season with a little salt and black pepper.

Stir the roast squash and onion mixture through the lentils mixture, then taste and adjust the seasoning, adding a little extra salt and black pepper, if necessary. Divide the mixture between 4 individual pie dishes, levelling it out, then spoon the mash over the top, spreading it level with the back of a fork and making sure the lentil mixture is covered completely. Dot a little extra butter over the surface.

Bake in the oven for around 20 minutes or until crispy on top and bubbling hot. Serve hot. Packed full of vegetables, these pies don't really need anything to serve alongside, but you may like to add a little greenery in the form of some steamed cabbage or broccoli, or a mixed green salad on a summery day.

Homity Pie

I remember often making this super frugal pie during my slightly impoverished student days, always following the recipe from my well-thumbed Cranks Vegetarian Cookbook. The book was lost or mislaid many years ago, but the memory of the pie stays firmly with me. In my student days, I always made it with wholemeal pastry, it being marginally more nutritious than standard shortcrust. Here, I make this version using a rye flour pastry and either are lovely, but I do think a purely white flour pastry might be a little at odds with its wholefood roots. The choice, however, is yours to make. Much like the Swede and Bacon Pie on page 70, the pastry here doesn't need blind-baking due to the robust filling.

Serves 4–6 | Takes 20 minutes to make (plus cooling), 1 hour 20 minutes to cook

1kg floury potatoes, peeled and cut into small (2–3cm) chunks
2 tbsp olive oil
25g unsalted butter
3 large onions, thinly sliced
couple of sprigs of fresh rosemary, leaves picked and chopped, and a few fresh sage leaves, chopped (or use 1 tsp dried mixed herbs)
3 cloves garlic, crushed
plain flour, for dusting
1 batch of Rye or Wholemeal Shortcrust Pastry or use 1 batch of standard Shortcrust Pastry (see pages 6–7), if you prefer
175g mature Cheddar cheese, grated
salt and freshly ground black pepper

Cook the potatoes in a large pan of lightly salted boiling water until tender, around 10–15 minutes, depending on the size you cut them. Drain well and set aside.

Meanwhile, put the oil and butter into a large, deep frying pan and set over a low heat. Once the butter has melted, stir through the onions and herbs and cook very gently, uncovered, for around 30–40 minutes or until very soft and lightly caramelised, stirring occasionally. You are not looking to colour the onions much at all, just render them to a sweet soft mass, so going slowly is absolutely necessary. Add the garlic and cook for a further couple of minutes before tipping in the cooked potatoes, mashing gently with the back of a wooden spoon to break them up a bit. Season well with salt and freshly ground black pepper and then set aside to cool completely.

Once the filling is cold, preheat the oven to 200°C/180°C fan/gas 6. Set a heavy baking sheet on a shelf in the oven to heat up.

On a lightly floured work surface, roll out the pastry of your choice to a thickness of about 3mm and use it to line a 23cm springform cake tin, bringing it about 4cm up the sides of the tin. Stir about two-thirds of the cheese through the cold potato mixture and then pile it into the pastry case, spreading evenly. Sprinkle over the remaining cheese and then carefully slide the tin onto the hot baking sheet in the oven. Bake for around 40 minutes or until the pastry is cooked and the top is golden brown and lightly crisp.

Remove from the oven and leave to cool for a few minutes before sliding a knife around the inside edge of the tin and releasing the springform. Carefully transfer the pie to a serving plate or wooden board. Serve hot or warm with a couple of interesting mixed salads or some seasonal green veg. I also like to eat this with some spicy chutney to give it a bit of zing.

Cauliflower Cheese and Mustard Tarts

I love cauliflower cheese, it's such a comforting treat, but it does lack a little in the crunch department. Some may say that's the whole point, but I like a bit of contrasting texture when I eat. So my solution here is to put the cauliflower cheese in a pie case and top it with a sprinkling of herby croutons, making it, to my mind, just a little bit more interesting. Just don't fill the pastry cases until you are ready to eat or they will go soggy, which rather defeats the whole point.

Serves 4 | Takes 25 minutes to make (plus chilling), 25 minutes to cook

For the pastry cases and croutons
plain flour, for dusting
1 batch of Shortcrust Pastry (see pages 6–7)
2 thick slices bread from a fresh wholemeal loaf
2 tbsp olive oil
1 tsp dried mixed herbs
salt and freshly ground black pepper

For the cauliflower cheese
1 large cauliflower (about 1.2kg), cut into florets (or use 2 smaller cauliflowers)
60g butter
60g plain flour
700ml milk
100–150g mature Cheddar cheese (to taste), grated
2 tsp wholegrain mustard

To make the pastry cases, lightly dust some flour over the work surface and cut the pastry into 4 equal-size pieces, gently rolling each one into a ball. Roll out each ball to a thickness of about 3mm and use it to line an individual deep loose-based tart tin (about 12cm diameter), pressing well into the base and up the sides of the tin. Take the rolling pin and give it a swift roll across the top of each tin, neatly trimming off the excess pastry, then pinch around with your thumb and forefinger to squeeze the pastry just a little higher than the top of the tins (a couple of millimetres or so) – this will allow for a little shrinkage as it cooks and creates a nice neat finish. Chill in the fridge for 20 minutes.

Meanwhile, preheat the oven 200°C/180°C fan/gas 6.

Place the tins on a baking sheet and line each one with non-stick baking paper and baking beans (see page 10 for more tips on blind-baking). Bake in the oven for 15 minutes. Remove the paper and beans, then bake for a further 5 minutes to cook the pastry through completely. Remove from the oven and set aside.

Whilst the pastry cases are baking, make the croutons. Cut the crusts off the bread and discard, then cut the bread into 1cm cubes and spread out over a baking sheet. Drizzle over the oil and then sprinkle over the herbs and a seasoning of salt and freshly ground black pepper. Slide into the oven alongside the pastry cases and bake for 10–15 minutes or until crisp and lightly browned. Remove from the oven and set aside.

Meanwhile, make the cauliflower cheese. Cook the cauliflower in a large saucepan of lightly salted boiling water for around 15–20 minutes or until tender, depending on the size of the florets. Drain well and leave in the colander for a few minutes to let the steam evaporate off.

In the meantime, melt the butter in a saucepan set over a medium heat. Sprinkle in the flour, stirring well to form a smooth paste or roux. Gradually pour in the milk, whisking all the time to prevent any lumps forming. Bring gently to the boil and then simmer steadily for about 5 minutes until the sauce is smooth and thickened. Reduce the heat to low and stir through the cheese and mustard, then season to taste with salt and black pepper. Finally, stir through the cooked cauliflower florets and reheat gently until piping hot throughout.

When you are ready to eat, carefully remove the baked pastry cases from the tins. Spoon the cauliflower cheese into the tart cases, dividing it evenly, and then sprinkle over the croutons. Serve immediately, perhaps with a bowlful of cooked peas or broccoli to eat alongside.

Celery and Cheddar Double-crust Pie

I don't know if celery has fallen slightly out of favour these days, but it's certainly something I seemed to eat more of as a child. Two things Mum made really stick in my mind, a sort of scone-bread made with cheese and celery and dusted heavily with paprika, and cream of celery soup. The cheese here is the linking theme, as Cheddar in particular is just such a great partner to the strong herbal flavour of celery. Here a generous layer of grated cheese is sandwiched between soft braised celery to make a very satisfying vegetarian pie.

Serves 2–3 | Takes 20 minutes to make (plus cooling), 1 hour 20 minutes to cook

50g unsalted butter
1 tbsp olive oil
2 onions, chopped
1 head celery, sliced
250ml vegetable stock
plain flour, for dusting
double batch of Shortcrust Pastry (see pages 6–7)
100g mature Cheddar cheese, grated
salt and freshly ground black pepper
a little beaten egg or a mixture of milk and vegetable oil, to glaze
sea salt flakes, for sprinkling

Melt the butter with the olive oil in a heavy-based saucepan. Add the onions and celery and cook over a medium-low heat for around 10 minutes or until they are just starting to soften. Season generously with salt and freshly ground black pepper and then pour in the stock. Bring to the boil, then reduce the heat and simmer, uncovered, for around 30 minutes or until the celery is really soft and the stock has virtually all evaporated, stirring every now and then. Remove from the heat and leave to cool completely.

Once the filling is cold, preheat the oven to 200°C/180°C fan/gas 6 and place a heavy baking sheet on a shelf in the oven to heat up.

On a lightly floured work surface, cut the pastry into 2 pieces, making one piece slightly larger than the other. Roll out the larger piece to a thickness of about 3mm and use it to line a deep pie plate (about 22–23cm in diameter).

Spoon half of the filling into the pastry case, levelling it a little with the back of the spoon, sprinkle over the cheese, then top with the rest of the filling, spreading it evenly. Brush the rim of the pastry with a little cold water to dampen it. Roll out the other piece of pastry so it is slightly bigger than the top of the pie plate and lay it over the filling, pressing down firmly onto the bottom piece of pastry to seal the edges. Crimp the edges if you like. Make a couple of slits in the top of the pie to let the steam out. Glaze with a little beaten egg or a mixture of milk and oil and sprinkle over a few sea salt flakes.

Carefully slide the pie onto the hot baking sheet in the oven and bake for about 40 minutes or until the pastry is golden brown, crisp and cooked through. Serve hot or warm. Something green is good here as an accompaniment – perhaps mixed green vegetables in the winter and a green salad in the summer.

Spiced Parsnip Tart

I love the interesting flavour of parsnips and often try to find ways of using them other than the obligatory Sunday roast variety. They are cheap and cheerful too, making them easy on the wallet. Their natural sweetness is perfectly offset by a few spices, in this case an Indian-style blend of mustard seeds, cumin and turmeric. Replace some or all of the milk with single cream if you are feeling a little more indulgent or happen to have some to use up. I like to eat this tart warm with a dollop of bringal pickle, a pungently spicy aubergine chutney.

Serves 4 | Takes to 20 minutes to make, 50 minutes to cook

2 tbsp sunflower or vegetable oil
1 onion, finely chopped
2 tsp mustard seeds
2 tsp cumin seeds
1/2 tsp ground turmeric
a pinch of dried chilli flakes
800g parsnips (about 9–10 smallish ones or 6 large ones), peeled and grated
small bunch of fresh coriander, chopped
1 deep 25cm blind-baked Shortcrust Pastry Tart Case (see pages 6–7)
3 eggs
200ml milk or single cream
75g mature Cheddar cheese, grated
salt and freshly ground black pepper

Heat the oil in a large, deep frying pan, then add the onion and fry over a medium-high heat for around 5 minutes. The onion should be starting to soften and colour just a little at the edges. Stir through the mustard and cumin seeds, the turmeric, chilli flakes and a seasoning of salt and freshly ground black pepper, then fry for a further minute. Reduce the heat a little and add the grated parsnips – don't worry if the volume looks a little alarming, it will cook down. Cook, uncovered, for about 10–15 minutes or until the parsnip has wilted and is softening, stirring occasionally.

Preheat the oven to 200°C/180°C fan/gas 6.

Stir the coriander through the parsnip mixture and taste. You may need to add a little more salt to offset the sweetness of the parsnips. Spoon the parsnip mixture into the pastry tart case, levelling a little but not pressing down too much or you will compact the mixture, making it hard for the custard to fill the gaps.

In a jug or small mixing bowl, whisk together the eggs and milk. Slowly pour into the pastry tart case, allowing time for it to seep through and find its own space around the parsnip. If you pour it in all in one go it's likely to overflow. Finally, sprinkle over the cheese.

Bake in the oven for around 30 minutes or until just set. Carefully remove the tart from the tin and place it on a serving plate or wooden board. Serve hot or warm. This tart is nice served with some Indian-inspired salads. A combination of red onion, fresh coriander and cucumber, dressed in a lemon and mustard seed dressing, will provide a good sharp contrast to the spicy sweetness of the tart.

Storecupboard Vegetable Pies

These pies emerged from what can only be described as mild desperation – a Friday night creation after a long week, when no one had an ounce of energy to go to the shops. Sometimes it amazes me that on a second glance my cupboards are not quite as bare as I imagined. The cans of borlotti beans and sweetcorn can be swapped for other beans or canned vegetables, if you like, although I do think sweetcorn is the most successful of the canned veg and I always have a couple of cans handy. The frozen peas can be substituted with frozen soya or green beans, and the dried thyme for oregano or mixed herbs. In essence, whatever you find lurking.

Makes 2 individual pies (easily scaled up to feed more) | Takes 20 minutes to make (plus cooling), 35 minutes to cook

30g butter
30g plain flour, plus extra for dusting
300ml milk
1 clove garlic, crushed
a pinch of dried thyme, plus extra for sprinkling
1 tsp (or more to taste) mustard, such as Dijon, English or wholegrain
400g can borlotti beans (or other canned beans), drained and rinsed
198g can sweetcorn kernels, drained
a large handful of frozen peas
75g mature Cheddar cheese, grated
$1/3$ pack (165g) ready-made puff pastry
salt and freshly ground black pepper
a little beaten egg or 1 tbsp milk mixed with 1 tbsp vegetable oil, to glaze

To make the filling, melt the butter in a heavy-based saucepan set over a medium heat and then stir through the flour to form a smooth paste or roux. Gradually pour in the milk, stirring all the time to prevent any lumps forming as the sauce begins to thicken. Bring gently to the boil and then simmer steadily for about 5 minutes to cook the flour. Add the garlic, thyme and mustard, season with salt and freshly ground black pepper, then cook for a further minute or two. Remove from the heat, then stir through the beans, sweetcorn, peas and cheese. Divide between 2 individual pie dishes and set aside to cool completely.

Once the filling is cold, preheat the oven to 220°C/200°C fan/gas 7.

On a lightly floured work surface, cut the pastry in half and then roll out each piece to a thickness of about 3mm to fit the pie dishes. Brush the rim of each pie dish with a little cold water and lay a piece of pastry over the filling in each dish, pressing down firmly at the edges to seal. Trim the edges with a small sharp knife, then crimp them if you like. Cut a slit in the top of each pie, brushing over a little beaten egg or the mixed milk and oil to glaze. Sprinkle over a little more thyme.

Bake in the oven for around 20–25 minutes or until the pastry is cooked and the filling is bubbling hot. Serve hot. I'm not sure these pies need much of an accompaniment, being an odds and sods sort of dish. An extra bowl of cooked peas won't go amiss if you are feeling like more of the healthy stuff.

Moroccan Carrot Tart Tatin

I made this tart when I had a glut of carrots in the fridge, one of those giant bags that are irresistibly cheap in the supermarket. The sweetness of carrots works very well with spices. All spices taste fresher if you use them whole and grind them yourself, and cumin in particular benefits from a quick toast in a dry frying pan to bring its heady scent alive. The quick yogurt dressing for serving provides a sharp contrast that stops the tart being too sweet.

Serves 3–4 | Takes 20 minutes to make (plus cooling), 40 minutes to cook

For the tart tatin
500g carrots, peeled and sliced
1 heaped tsp cumin seeds
1 heaped tsp coriander seeds
1/2 tsp Spanish smoked paprika
1/2 tsp ground cinnamon
50g unsalted butter
1 tbsp sherry vinegar
1 tsp runny honey
plain flour, for dusting
1/2 pack (250g) ready-made puff pastry
salt and freshly ground black pepper
chopped fresh coriander, to garnish

For the yogurt dressing
2–3 tbsp natural yogurt (I use Greek-style yogurt for extra richness)
1 clove garlic, crushed
loose handful of fresh coriander, chopped
squeeze of lemon juice, to taste

To make the tart tatin, plunge the carrots into a pan of lightly salted boiling water and blanch for 5 minutes or until just tender but with plenty of bite. Drain well and set aside.

Put the whole spices into a medium-size (about 23cm diameter) ovenproof frying pan and toast over a medium-high heat for a couple of minutes. As soon as you smell their aroma wafting up from the pan, remove from the heat and tip the spices into a pestle and mortar, then roughly grind. Stir in the paprika and cinnamon.

Add the butter to the same frying pan, then leave it to melt over a low heat before tipping the ground spices back in, along with some salt and freshly ground black pepper. Add the drained carrots, stirring well, and fry for a few minutes to allow the carrots to absorb some of the buttery juices. Add the sherry vinegar and honey and fry for a further minute. Turn off the heat, spread the carrots out in an even single layer over the bottom of the pan and set aside to cool completely.

Whilst the carrots are cooling, make the yogurt dressing by mixing the yogurt, garlic and coriander together in a small bowl. Season to taste with lemon juice and salt and black pepper. Set aside in the fridge.

Once the carrots are cold, preheat the oven to 220°C/200°C fan/gas 7.

On a lightly floured work surface, roll out the pastry to a thickness of about 3mm. Cut it into a round that is just a little bigger than the diameter of the frying pan. Lay the pastry over the carrots, tucking it snugly around the edge of the carrots, down around the inside of the pan.

Bake in the oven for around 25 minutes or until the pastry is crisp, golden and cooked through. Remove from the oven and leave to cool for a minute or so before carefully inverting the tart onto a serving plate or wooden board. Garnish with a sprinkling of chopped coriander and serve hot or warm. Drizzle over the chilled yogurt dressing just before serving.

This tart is nice served with fluffy couscous, perhaps with a few chopped fresh herbs, dried apricots and toasted almonds stirred through.

Melting Onion Tart

This is perhaps my very favourite tart in the world. It's basically just onions in a pastry tart case, but the onions are cooked so slowly over a long, long period of time, that they take on an incredibly sweet flavour and an almost melting texture. You can make it even more frugal by replacing the cream with all milk, but I must admit, a little cream does work wonders here.

Serves 6 | Takes 20 minutes to make (plus cooling), 1 hour 40 minutes to cook

50g unsalted butter
1 tbsp olive oil
900g onions, peeled and sliced (about 5–6 large or 8–9 medium ones)
2 sprigs of fresh rosemary, leaves picked and finely chopped
1 deep 25cm blind-baked Shortcrust Pastry Tart Case (see pages 6–7)
150ml double cream
150ml milk
3 eggs
salt and freshly ground black pepper

Put the butter and oil into a deep, wide frying pan and melt together very gently. Stir in the onions and rosemary. Tear off a sheet of greaseproof paper big enough to cover the onions, scrunch up and briefly rinse under running water. Shake off the excess water and then cover the onions with the dampened paper, tucking the paper down the edges so that it sits within the frying pan. This creates a steamy lid that'll help the onions soften without colouring too much. Cook the covered onions as gently as possible and for as long as possible (an hour or so is ideal if you have the time), lifting the paper to stir once or twice. Remove from the heat, discard the paper and set aside to cool a little.

Preheat the oven to 200°C/180°C fan/gas 6.

Spoon the onion mixture into the pastry tart case and spread evenly. In a bowl, lightly beat the cream, milk and eggs together, then season with a little salt and plenty of freshly ground black pepper. Slowly pour into the pastry tart case, allowing it to settle and find its own level gradually around the filling.

Bake in the oven for around 35–40 minutes or until the filling is just set and golden brown. Carefully remove the tart from the tin and place it on a serving plate or wooden board. Serve hot, or even better, warm, when the flavour of the sweet onions will really shine through. A crisp green salad with plenty of fresh herbs is my ideal accompaniment.

Wild Garlic, Leek and Blue Cheese Quiche

So frugal as it's completely free, wild garlic is a wonderfully satisfying thing to forage and cook with. Starting in early spring, this leafy vegetable is surprisingly easy to find, so if you have even a small wood near you it's worth a look. You won't be able to miss its pungent odour, and it's the strap-like leaves you pick, although the flowers are also edible and very pretty scattered over salads. Treat the leaves just as you would spinach. They are wonderful sautéed and stirred through pasta or even made into a filling for ravioli – in this recipe they make a lovely rich and subtly garlicky quiche.

Serves 4 | Takes 15 minutes to make, 50 minutes to cook

2 tbsp olive oil
2 leeks, washed and sliced
150g (about 4 handfuls) wild garlic, washed well, drained and roughly chopped
1 shallow 25cm blind-baked Shortcrust Pastry Tart Case (see pages 6–7)
200g crème fraîche
2 eggs
100g blue cheese (such as Stilton, or a similar creamy blue), crumbled
salt and freshly ground black pepper

Put the oil into a large, deep frying pan set over a low heat and heat gently, then stir in the leeks. Scrunch up a sheet of greaseproof paper and briefly rinse it under running water. Shake off the excess water, then lay the dampened paper over the leeks, tucking it under snugly at the edges. This creates a steamy lid that will help the leeks soften without colouring. Sweat the leeks gently for around 15 minutes or until they are soft and tender, lifting the paper to stir occasionally.

Preheat the oven to 200°C/180°C fan/gas 6.

Add the wild garlic to the leeks, then re-cover loosely with the paper and cook for a further 5–8 minutes or until the garlic has wilted. Remove from the heat, discard the paper, then spoon this softened filling into the pastry tart case and spread evenly. Set aside.

In a jug, whisk together the crème fraîche and eggs, seasoning well with salt and freshly ground black pepper. Slowly pour into the pastry tart case, allowing it to find its own level among the vegetables. Finally, scatter over the blue cheese.

Bake in the oven for around 25–30 minutes or until the filling is just set. Carefully remove the quiche from the tin to a serving plate or wooden board. Serve hot or warm. This is a rich and creamy quiche, so something crunchy and robust in flavour, like a rocket and Little Gem salad, will be good to serve alongside.

Red Onion Tart Tatin with Sage and Parmesan Pastry

This upside-down tart is a great vegetarian treat for a weekend lunch or supper. Whilst it's a pretty frugal affair cost-wise, the onions take a little time, love and patience to cook right, so this is probably not a dish to tackle on a weeknight.

Serves 2–3 | Takes 20 minutes to make (plus cooling), 1 hour 10 minutes to cook

2 tbsp olive oil
3 large red onions, cut into 8 wedges through the root
1 tbsp caster sugar
1 tbsp balsamic vinegar
25g unsalted butter, cut into little cubes
plain flour, for dusting
1 batch of Sage and Parmesan Rough Puff Pastry (see pages 7–8)
salt and freshly ground black pepper
fresh Parmesan cheese shavings, to garnish

Pour the oil into a medium-size (about 23cm diameter) ovenproof frying pan and set over a really low heat. Spread the onion wedges out in a snugly-packed single layer, placing them in the pan with one of the cut-sides down. Scrunch up a sheet of greaseproof paper and briefly rinse it under running water. Shake off the excess water, then lay the dampened paper over the onions, tucking it under snugly at the edges. This creates a steamy lid that will help the onions soften without colouring. Cook without turning for 20 minutes, giving the pan a little shake back and forth once or twice to check the onions aren't sticking. Carefully turn the onions over onto the other cut-sides, using a fork and palette knife to help you, keeping the onions spread in a single layer. Re-cover with the damp paper (dampening the paper again with a little more water, if necessary) and cook for a further 15 minutes.

Remove the paper once again, then evenly sprinkle over the sugar and balsamic vinegar and dot on the cubes of butter. Turn the onions once more – it will be a little trickier this time as they will be pretty soft – then re-cover with the damp paper and cook for a final 10 minutes. Turn off the heat, discard the paper and season generously with salt and freshly

ground black pepper. Set aside to cool completely.

Once the onions are cold, preheat the oven to 220°C/200°C fan/gas 7.

On a lightly floured work surface, roll out the pastry to a thickness of about 3mm. Cut it into a round that is just a little bigger than the diameter of the frying pan. Lay the pastry over the onions, tucking it snugly around the edge of the onions, down around the inside of the pan.

Bake in the oven for around 25 minutes or until the pastry is crisp, golden and cooked through. Remove from the oven and leave to cool for a minute or so before carefully inverting the tart onto a serving plate or wooden board. Garnish with shavings of Parmesan and serve hot or warm with a generous green salad to accompany.

Savoy Cabbage and Hazelnut Strudels

I know a cabbage strudel might sound just a little bit too frugal, but believe me, this dish equates to more than the sum of its minimal ingredients. Cabbage, cooked properly, has to be one of my favourite vegetables and here it is gently sautéed to softness with a little butter and seasonings. So simple, but trust me, it's delicious. The hazelnuts are there to add a bit of healthy crunch, the cheese to add just a little richness. Don't feel constrained by my choice of nuts and cheese though – this is a good recipe for using up odds and sods of cheese, and those half packets of stale nuts that always seem to be left over from baking recipes. A little toast in a dry pan will also bring the nuts back to life in an instant.

Makes 2 strudels (each serving 2) | Takes 25 minutes to make (plus cooling), 1 hour 5 minutes to cook

50g hazelnuts
50g unsalted butter
650g Savoy cabbage, washed and finely shredded
1 pack (250g) filo pastry (about 10 sheets)
30–50g butter, melted
100g Gruyère cheese, grated
salt and freshly ground black pepper

Set a large frying pan over a medium heat and add the hazelnuts, then dry-fry for a few minutes or until they are nicely toasted. Remove from the heat, tip the hazelnuts onto a board and roughly chop, then set aside.

Reduce the heat a little and add the unsalted butter to the pan, allowing it to melt. Stir through the slightly damp shredded cabbage and season well with salt and freshly ground black pepper. Cover with a lid or snug-fitting piece of foil and cook gently for around 20–25 minutes or until soft to the bite. Remove from the heat and set aside to cool completely – spreading the mixture out on a shallow tray will speed this up considerably.

Once the filling is cold, preheat the oven to 200°C/180°C fan/gas 6.

Unroll the stack of filo pastry sheets onto the work surface. Lift up half of the pastry sheets (keeping them together in a stack), then cover the rest with a clean damp tea towel to prevent them drying out.

Take 1 sheet of filo (from the first stack) and brush it lightly with a little melted butter, then lay another sheet directly on top. Brush that sheet with a little melted butter and lay another sheet on top as before, then keep going in the same way, layering the sheets of filo on top of each other, until you have used all 5 sheets.

Lift the stack of filo pastry sheets onto a baking sheet and spoon half of the cabbage mixture down the middle. Sprinkle over half of the toasted hazelnuts and half of the cheese. Fold over one side to cover the filling, brush the top of the folded pastry with a little more melted butter, then fold the other side over to seal the cabbage filling inside, sticking it down onto the butter. Brush all over with a little more melted butter, then turn the short ends over, sticking them firmly down – you will be left with a large sausage roll shape with the cabbage filling completely encased in pastry. Carefully roll it over so that the stuck edges are now all underneath and brush the top with a final slick of melted butter.

Repeat with the remaining sheets of filo pastry, melted butter, cabbage mixture, hazelnuts and cheese (assembling the strudel on a separate baking sheet) to make 2 separate strudels.

Bake both strudels in the oven for around 30–35 minutes or until cooked, crisp and golden. Serve hot. These strudels are best served immediately whilst the pastry is crisp and the filling bubbling. The pastry has a tendency to go a little soggy with time. Buttered new potatoes served alongside will be a nice accompaniment for these strudels.

Potato and Smoked Mackerel Pie

Packs of smoked mackerel are really good value, and with such a strong punchy flavour you don't need much per person to make a very tasty meal. Being a bit of a pepper fiend, I always buy the ones crusted in crushed black peppercorns, but use the plain ones if you prefer. Mackerel is also one of our most sustainable fish sources, so they score pretty highly on the eco front too.

Serves 4 | Takes 20 minutes to make, 1 hour to cook

2 tbsp olive oil
25g unsalted butter
3 onions, sliced
1.2kg floury potatoes, peeled and cut into 1cm-thick slices
2 cloves garlic, crushed
250g smoked mackerel fillets, peppered or plain, skinned and flaked
4 tbsp crème fraîche
2 tbsp horseradish sauce
300ml fish or vegetable stock
75g mature Cheddar cheese, grated
salt and freshly ground black pepper

Put the oil and butter into a large frying pan and set over a medium-low heat. Once the butter has melted, stir through the onions and cook slowly, uncovered, for about 30 minutes or until they are soft and lightly caramelised, stirring every now and then.

Meanwhile, cook the potato slices in a large pan of lightly salted boiling water for around 12–15 minutes or until tender. Drain well.

Add the garlic to the onion mixture and cook for a further minute. Remove from the heat and stir through the cooked potatoes and flaked mackerel.

Preheat the oven to 200°C/180°C fan/gas 6.

Put the crème fraîche and horseradish sauce into a small mixing bowl and gradually pour in the stock, whisking as you go so it comes together as a smooth sauce. Season well with salt and freshly ground black pepper. Pour the sauce over the potato mixture and lightly fold through so it is evenly mixed, but try not to break up the potatoes and fish too much. Spoon into a baking dish and spread evenly, then sprinkle over the cheese.

Bake in the oven for around 30 minutes or until the top is lightly golden and bubbling. Serve hot with a big green salad – a mix of delicious, peppery watercress leaves and spinach are ideal.

CHICKEN

Leftover Chicken Pie

This tasty pie is made just for two, as that was the amount of leftover chicken I happened to have to hand when I was making it. It can, of course, be doubled if you have more meat available, or it can even be made with uncooked chicken – diced thigh meat is my preference for flavour. Add it along with the chicken stock and simmer for 10 minutes or so to cook it through, before adding the peas and continuing.

Serves 2 (generously) | Takes 20 minutes to make (plus cooling), 1 hour 10 minutes to cook

1 tbsp olive oil
25g unsalted butter
1 onion, chopped
1 carrot, chopped
1 stick celery, chopped
a pinch of dried mixed herbs (optional)
1 heaped tbsp plain flour, plus extra for dusting
300ml chicken stock
a large handful of frozen peas
200g leftover cold cooked chicken, shredded
double batch of Shortcrust Pastry (see pages 6–7)
salt and freshly ground black pepper
a little beaten egg or a mixture of milk and vegetable oil, to glaze

Put the olive oil and butter into a heavy-based saucepan and set over a low heat until melted. Tip in the onion, carrot, celery, herbs and a good seasoning of salt and freshly ground black pepper. Stir well to coat and then allow the vegetables to soften gently without colouring for around 20 minutes, stirring occasionally.

Sprinkle in the flour and stir it thoroughly through the vegetables, allowing it to cook for a minute or two. Gradually pour in the stock, stirring all the time to prevent any lumps forming as the sauce begins to thicken. Increase the heat a little and bring to the boil, then simmer steadily for about 5 minutes to cook the flour. Stir through the peas, then remove from the heat and leave to cool completely. Once cold, stir through the cooked chicken.

Once the filling is cold, preheat the oven to 200°C/180°C fan/gas 6 and place a heavy baking sheet on a shelf in the oven to heat up.

On a lightly floured work surface, cut the pastry into 2 pieces, making one piece slightly larger than the other. Roll out the larger piece to a thickness of about 3mm and use it to line a deep pie plate (about 22–23cm in diameter).

Spoon the filling into the pastry case, levelling it a little with the back of the spoon. Brush the rim of the pastry with a little cold water to dampen it. Roll out the other piece of pastry so it is slightly bigger than the top of the pie plate and lay it over the filling, pressing down firmly onto the bottom piece of pastry to seal the edges. Crimp the edges if you like. Make a couple of slits in the top of the pie to let the steam out and glaze with a little beaten egg or a mixture of milk and oil.

Carefully slide the pie onto the hot baking sheet in the oven and bake for about 40 minutes or until the pastry is crisp, golden brown and cooked through. Serve hot. As with all these classic pies, a bit of mashed potato is good to serve alongside. Or, if you have leftover roast potatoes and greens, as well as the roast chicken, you can fry them up with a little olive oil for a simple bubble and squeak.

Roast Chicken, Sweet Potato and Mozzarella Tart

This tart began life as a true 'leftovers' meal – a quick, tasty way of using up cold roast chicken and roast sweet potatoes and combining them with half a pack of puff pastry and a handful of black olives. I love tossing chunks of sweet potato or butternut squash in olive oil and roasting them around a chicken – they seem to soak up the delicious meaty juices beautifully. Just add them around your bird about halfway through cooking to make sure they don't overcook.

Serves 3–4 | Takes 15 minutes to make, 25 minutes to cook

plain flour, for dusting
$1/2$ pack (250g) ready-made puff pastry
400g cold roast sweet potatoes, cut into chunks
200g cold roast chicken, torn into bite-size pieces
1 ball (125g) fresh mozzarella, drained and torn into bite-size pieces
handful of stoned black olives, drained (about 75g)
3–4 sprigs of fresh rosemary, leaves picked
salt and freshly ground black pepper

Preheat the oven to 220°C/200°C fan/gas 7.

On a lightly floured work surface, roll out the pastry into a rough square or rectangle about 3mm thick to fit a large baking sheet. Using a sharp knife, trim the edges straight – this will help the pastry puff up in the oven. Line the base of a baking sheet with non-stick baking paper (if the baking sheet has a tendency to stick) and carefully lift the pastry onto the baking sheet, using the rolling pin to support it as you do so. Using the tip of a sharp knife, score a shallow line about 1cm in from the edge all the way around the edge of the pastry, to create a border – this will help the pastry to puff up at the edges.

Scatter over the sweet potatoes, chicken and mozzarella, keeping them inside the border. Tuck the olives into the gaps and sprinkle over the rosemary leaves. Season generously with salt and freshly ground black pepper.

Bake in the oven for 20–25 minutes or until puffed up and golden. Served hot with a crisp green salad dressed in a punchy dressing, this makes a great lunch or supper dish.

Pasta Pie with Tomato, Tuna and Cheese

OK, so this is just a simple supper of pasta shapes with a rich tomato and tuna sauce, but you have to admit it does look pretty impressive, the rigatoni tubes all standing up straight as soldiers. When you are making it you will be very disbelieving, but it really does all stay together when you unleash it from its tin. Lining up the pasta is a tiny bit time-consuming, but it's definitely child's play so why not rope in a few small paws to lend a hand? With my kids at least, the more I get them to do, the more likely they seem to be to try something new. That's the theory anyway.

Serves 4–6 | Takes 30 minutes to make, 1 hour 10 minutes to cook

2 tbsp olive oil, plus a little extra for greasing and for the cooked pasta
2 onions, chopped
3 cloves garlic, crushed
2 x 400g cans chopped tomatoes
2 tbsp tomato purée
1 tsp granulated sugar
500g dried rigatoni (fat tubes)
2 x 200g cans tuna, drained
small bunch of fresh basil, chopped
2 x 125g balls fresh mozzarella, drained and diced into 1cm cubes
40g fresh Parmesan cheese, finely grated
salt and freshly ground black pepper

Grease a 23cm springform cake tin well with oil and set aside.

Pour the oil into a large saucepan, add the onions and fry over a medium heat for around 10 minutes or until starting to soften and colour just a little at the edges. Stir through the garlic and fry for just a minute before pouring in the tomatoes, then stir through the tomato purée and sugar. Season well with salt and freshly ground black pepper. Bring to a simmer, then simmer steadily, uncovered, for about 35–40 minutes or until thick and almost jam-like, stirring occasionally.

Meanwhile, bring a large pan of lightly salted water to a rolling boil. Add the pasta, giving it a few stirs to stop it clumping together, and bring it back to the boil. Cook for 12 minutes or so until tender but with plenty of bite – it will cook a little further on baking. Drain well, return to the pan and drizzle in a little oil to keep the tubes from sticking together, then leave to cool slightly.

Preheat the oven to 200°C/180°C fan/gas 6.

Once the tomato sauce has thickened, turn off the heat and lightly fold through the tuna and basil, trying not to break the fish up too much as it's nice to have a bit of texture. Rest the prepared springform tin on a baking sheet to catch any drips, then pour in about half of the sauce, levelling with a spoon.

Now for the slightly fiddly bit – starting with a circle around the outside, butted right up to the springform, line up some pasta tubes vertically (open-end upwards), packing them tightly together. Continue lining up the pasta tubes in concentric circles as close together as possible until the whole tin is full of pasta tubes standing upright. Carefully pour the rest of the sauce evenly over the pasta. Sprinkle over the mozzarella cubes and grated Parmesan.

Bake in the oven for around 20 minutes or until the cheese has melted and crisped up on top. Remove from the oven and leave to cool for a couple of minutes or so. Release the springform and carefully remove the sides of the tin, then transfer the pie (keeping it on the base of the tin) to a serving plate or wooden board. Serve hot or warm on its own, or go the whole hog and add garlic bread and salad if you're feeding a hungry crowd.

Spiced Minced Beef and Potato Free-form Pie

In this easy-peasy free-form pie, I've spiced up minced beef with my favourite combination of cumin and smoked paprika. By good-quality minced beef I mean mince with a good fat content, because fat really equals flavour – minced beef with 20% fat is ideal, and I try to buy it from a butcher whom I know well enough.

Serves 4–6 | Takes 25 minutes to make (plus cooling), 1 hour 5 minutes to cook

1 heaped tbsp cumin seeds
1 tbsp olive oil
500g minced beef (preferably 20% fat)
1 tsp ground cinnamon
1 tsp Spanish smoked paprika
$^{1}/_{2}$ tsp ground turmeric
2 cloves garlic, crushed
hot chilli sauce, to taste
200ml beef stock
750g floury potatoes, peeled and cut into 5mm-thick slices
plain flour, for dusting
double batch of Rough Puff Pastry (see pages 7–8)
small bunch of fresh flat-leaf parsley, chopped
salt and freshly ground black pepper
1 egg, beaten, or 1 tbsp milk mixed with 1 tbsp vegetable oil, to glaze
a few sea salt flakes, for sprinkling

Put the cumin seeds into a deep frying pan set over a medium-high heat and toast for just a minute or two until their aroma wafts up from the pan. Add the olive oil and minced beef to the pan, stirring quickly to break up the meat and mix in the cumin seeds. Stir through the rest of the spices – the cinnamon, smoked paprika and turmeric – and fry for about 10 minutes or until the meat has crisped up a little at the edges. Add the garlic, then add some hot chilli sauce to taste, and season with salt and freshly ground black pepper. Pour in the stock and bring to the boil, then reduce the heat and simmer for about 5 minutes to reduce the stock a little. Remove from the heat and set aside to cool completely.

Meanwhile, cook the sliced potatoes in a large pan of lightly salted boiling water for 8–10 minutes or until just tender. Drain well and set aside to cool completely.

Once the mince mixture and the potatoes are cold, preheat the oven to 220°C/200°C fan/gas 7.

On a lightly floured work surface, cut the pastry into two-thirds and one-third, rolling each piece gently into a ball as you do so. Roll out the larger piece into a rough circle about 3mm thick. Transfer to a large baking sheet. Arrange the potatoes in overlapping circles over the pastry, starting from the outside but leaving a generous 5cm border all around the edges. Sprinkle over the chopped parsley and season with a little salt and black pepper. Spoon the spiced minced beef mixture over the top, again keeping it within the clear border around the edges.

Roll out the other piece of pastry so that it just about covers the filling, again to a thickness of about 3mm, and lay it over the top. Bring up the pastry border to meet the top piece of pastry and crimp the edges all around, brushing the join with a little cold water to help it seal. Cut a couple of slits in the top of the pie to let the steam out and brush all over with a little beaten egg or the mixture of milk and oil. Sprinkle a few sea salt flakes over the top.

Bake in the oven for around 45 minutes or until the pastry is crisp and deep golden brown. As this pie has no tin you have the advantage of being able to lift it a little with a fish slice to check the underside is cooked through. Serve hot or warm. I like to serve this pie with an interesting and colourful salad – perhaps a chopped cooked (cold) beetroot salad with plenty of chopped herbs, dressed in balsamic vinegar.

Beetroot, Feta, Bacon and Hazelnut Tarts

Ready-cooked beetroot (not in vinegar), the stuff that comes in vacuum packs, is a really useful thing to have. It lasts (almost) forever and can be used in dips, salads, soups and even sweet bakes, adding a lovely earthy note to chocolate cakes. The bacon in this recipe is not strictly essential, but it does add a pleasing savouriness to counterbalance the sweet beetroot. And besides, I often have a few rashers hanging around that need using up – the by-product of over-zealous shopping for the weekend's bacon sarnies. As for the herbs, I use rosemary as I have a bush outside the back door, but thyme (fresh or dried) is also a good alternative.

Makes 4 individual tarts | Takes 15 minutes to make, 25 minutes to cook

plain flour, for dusting
1/2 pack (250g) ready-made puff pastry
4 tbsp crème fraîche
couple of sprigs of fresh rosemary, leaves picked and roughly chopped
2 x 250g packs cooked beetroot (not in vinegar), sliced
200g feta cheese, crumbled
60g hazelnuts, roughly chopped
4 rashers streaky bacon, chopped (optional)
salt and freshly ground black pepper

Preheat the oven to 220°C/200°C fan/gas 7.

On a lightly floured work surface, roll out the pastry into a large rectangle about 3mm thick. Cut into 4 equal-size pieces and arrange on 2 baking sheets, making sure there is plenty of room around each one to give it room to rise. Using the tip of a sharp knife, score a shallow line about 1cm in from the edge all the way around the edge of each piece of pastry, to create a border – this will help the pastry to puff up at the edges.

In a small bowl, mix the crème fraîche with the rosemary and then season with a little salt and freshly ground black pepper. Divide the mixture between the pastry rectangles and spread evenly, keeping it within the borders. Divide the beetroot slices between the tarts and then scatter over the feta, hazelnuts and bacon, if using. Season with a generous grind of black pepper.

Bake in the oven for about 20–25 minutes or until the pastry is crisp and puffed up. Serve hot or warm. Salad is nice here as an accompaniment, something with a Mediterranean feel – ripe succulent tomatoes dressed with herbs and olive oil perhaps.

Leek, Bacon and Cheese Quiche

Easy, cheap and cheerful, this simple quiche makes a delicious lunch or light supper served with plenty of crunchy salad. And like all quiches it is a very adaptable beast – try swapping a few of the leeks for the same weight of sliced courgettes, peppers or sweetcorn kernels, replace the bacon with diced chorizo, or ring the changes with a different cheese.

Serves 4 | Takes 15 minutes to make, 55 minutes to cook

1 tbsp olive oil
150g smoked bacon lardons or chopped smoked streaky bacon rashers
600g leeks, washed and sliced
$1/2$ tsp dried thyme
1 deep 25cm blind-baked Shortcrust Pastry Tart Case (see pages 6–7)
200ml milk
2 large eggs
75g mature Cheddar cheese, grated
salt and freshly ground black pepper

Pour the oil into a large frying pan and set over a medium heat. Once the oil is hot, add the bacon and fry for about 5 minutes or until lightly crisp, stirring once or twice. If you stir too often, the temperature in the pan will be reduced and it will be harder to get nice crisp edges on the bacon, which will add flavour. Remove the bacon to a plate, then remove the pan from the heat and let it cool for a few minutes.

Set the pan back onto a low heat and add the leeks and thyme, then season with a little salt and plenty of freshly ground black pepper. Leeks burn easily and can turn a little bitter, so it's important not to cook them over too high a heat. Scrunch up a sheet of greaseproof paper and briefly rinse it under running water. Shake off the excess water and tuck the dampened paper over the leeks, then leave the leeks to sweat gently for about 15–20 minutes, lifting the paper to stir occasionally – you want the leeks to be soft and tender but not completely collapsing.

Preheat the oven to 200°C/180°C fan/gas 6.

Remove the pan from the heat, discard the paper and let the leek mixture cool slightly, before spooning it into the pastry tart case. Scatter the cooked bacon evenly over the top.

Measure the milk into a jug and beat in the eggs. Slowly pour into the pastry tart case, allowing it to settle and find its own level gradually around the filling – if you pour too fast, you risk it overflowing. Sprinkle over the cheese.

Bake in the oven for around 25–30 minutes or until the custard has set and the top is golden brown. Carefully remove the quiche from the tin to a serving plate or wooden board. Serve hot, warm or cold. A salad is always great with a quiche, so here I suggest perhaps adding a potato salad dressed Italian-style with oil, vinegar, chopped shallots and plenty of fresh herbs, plus a big green crunchy salad too.

Swede and Bacon Pie

This robust pie is filled with delicious buttery mashed swede, an underused vegetable that I think deserves a little more attention. The pastry case doesn't need to be blind-baked, as the filling is drier than the custard-based filling of a quiche so it won't go soggy. With a bottom crust pie like this one, it's always a good idea to preheat a heavy baking sheet in the oven to slide the tin onto, as the intense burst of bottom heat will help crisp up the base.

Serves 4–6 | Takes 20 minutes to make (plus cooling), 1 hour 10 minutes to cook

1.2kg swede (about 2 medium ones), peeled and cut into 2cm cubes
50g butter
a pinch of dried chilli flakes (optional)
freshly grated nutmeg, to taste
2 tbsp olive oil
1 large onion, chopped
200g smoked bacon lardons
plain flour, for dusting
1 batch of Shortcrust Pastry (see pages 6–7)
3 tbsp fresh breadcrumbs
75g mature Cheddar cheese, grated
salt and freshly ground black pepper

Cook the swede in a large pan of lightly salted boiling water until tender – this will perhaps take a little longer than you might imagine, around 25–30 minutes. Drain really well, then tip the swede back into the pan and allow the steam to evaporate off for a few minutes, before roughly mashing with the butter. Season to taste with salt and freshly ground black pepper, the chilli, if using, and nutmeg. Set aside.

Meanwhile, heat the oil in a frying pan set over a medium heat, add the onion and bacon lardons and fry for around 15 minutes or until golden, stirring frequently. Remove from the heat, stir through the mashed swede, then set aside to cool completely.

Once the filling is cold, preheat the oven to 200°C/180°C fan/gas 6. Set a heavy baking sheet on a shelf in the oven to heat up.

On a lightly floured work surface, roll out the pastry to a thickness of about 3mm and use it to line a 23cm springform cake tin, bringing it about 4cm up the sides of the tin. Don't worry about being too neat, this is a good pie for a bit of a rustic look!

Spoon the swede mixture into the pastry case, spreading it evenly. Sprinkle over the breadcrumbs and cheese and then carefully slide the tin onto the hot baking sheet in the oven. Bake for around 40 minutes or until the pastry is cooked and the cheesy topping is golden brown.

Remove from the oven and leave to cool for a few minutes before sliding a knife around the inside edge of the tin and releasing the springform. Carefully transfer the pie to a serving plate or wooden board. Serve hot. This frugal and simple pie is very nice just as it is but you can serve it with a dish of something green – like buttered cabbage or broccoli – if you want more.

Turkey, Ham, Spinach and Stilton Pie

A post-Christmas pie, originally made to use up the inevitable turkey leftovers, but this can easily be replaced with leftover roast chicken, if you prefer. I know I say it time and time again in my recipes (sometimes I feel like a stuck record), but the slow sweating of the onions is a really important step. Simply don't believe it when recipes tell you to sweat onions for 10 minutes until softened, as cooking an onion until properly soft takes at least double this. Reducing the onions to a sweet unctuous base for soups, stews or pie fillings takes even longer, so allow a minimum of 30 minutes to do it properly. Your patience will be rewarded with bags of delicious flavour.

Serves 4–6 | Takes 20 minutes to make (plus cooling), 1¼ hours to cook

25g unsalted butter
1 tbsp olive oil
2 large onions, chopped
2 cloves garlic, crushed
50g plain flour
400ml milk
200ml double cream (or extra milk)
¼ of a nutmeg, freshly grated
240g bag fresh spinach, washed and shaken well to dry
175g Stilton, crumbled
300g cold cooked turkey (or chicken) meat, diced
300g cold cooked ham, chopped
1 pack (320g) ready-rolled puff pastry (1 rectangular sheet)
salt and freshly ground black pepper
a little beaten egg or a mixture of milk and vegetable oil, to glaze

Melt the butter with the olive oil in a deep frying pan set over a low heat. Add the onions and cook gently, uncovered, until they are soft and sweet, stirring occasionally. Allow a minimum of 20 minutes, although 30 minutes is better if you have the time and patience. A layer of damp scrunched up greaseproof paper tucked over the onions creates a steamy lid that will help them soften gently without colouring.

Add the garlic and cook gently for a further minute before adding the flour. Stir well until the flour is completely combined with the buttery juices. Gradually pour in the milk and cream, stirring constantly to prevent any lumps forming as the sauce begins to thicken. Bring gently to the boil and then simmer steadily for about 5 minutes to cook the flour. Season well with the nutmeg and salt and freshly ground black pepper.

Add the spinach, packing it onto the surface of the sauce, then cover the pan with a lid and allow the spinach to wilt for a few minutes over a low heat. If it won't all fit in one go, do this in 2 batches, allowing the first batch to wilt before adding the second. Stir

through the Stilton until it has melted and then remove from the heat. Press a piece of cling film over the surface to prevent a skin forming and leave to cool completely. Once cold, stir through the turkey and ham, then spoon into a large pie dish.

Once the filling is cold, preheat the oven to 220°C/200°C fan/gas 7.

Brush the rim of the pie dish with a little cold water and then unroll the pastry over the filling, pressing down firmly at the edges to seal. If the pastry is slightly too small for the dish you have chosen, just roll it a touch thinner to get it to fit. Trim the pastry edges with a small sharp knife, cut a slit in the top of the pie to let the steam out and brush the surface with a little beaten egg or a mixture of milk and oil.

Bake in the oven for around 30–35 minutes or until the pastry is crisp and cooked through. Serve hot. This pie is another candidate for a mound of buttery mashed potato served alongside.

WEEKEND PIES

Some pies are simply best suited for weekend cooking, when you have more time and the inclination to savour the process of making them just as much as devouring the end result. Homemade rough puff pastry rich with butter, generous fillings laden with cream, wine and fresh herbs, or meat braised gently until it is falling-apart tender – these things are on occasions well worth the extra effort. These are the pie recipes to turn to when you are entertaining friends or you simply want to offer your loved ones something a little bit more special.

Leek and Gruyère Tarts with Walnut Pastry

These little tartlets make a lovely rich starter and the walnut pastry is pleasingly nutty. You can of course make one big tart for sharing if you don't have small tins or simply want a cut-able dish. If you are making a big tart, it is best to blind-bake the pastry case before adding the filling, following the instructions on page 10.

Makes 6 small individual tartlets (ideal for a starter) | Takes 25 minutes to make (plus chilling and cooling), 40 minutes to cook

plain flour, for dusting
1 batch of Walnut Shortcrust Pastry (see pages 6–7)
600g leeks, washed and trimmed
1 tbsp olive oil
25g unsalted butter
few small sprigs of fresh thyme
2 eggs
200ml single cream
140g Gruyère cheese, cut into thin slices
salt and freshly ground black pepper

Lightly dust some flour over the work surface and cut the pastry into 6 equal-size pieces, gently rolling each one into a ball. Roll out each ball to a thickness of about 3mm and use it to line an individual loose-based tartlet tin (about 10cm diameter and 2cm deep), pressing well into the base and up the sides of the tin. Take the rolling pin and give it a swift roll across the top of each tin, neatly trimming off the excess pastry, then pinch around with your thumb and forefinger to squeeze the pastry just a little higher than the top of the tins (a couple of millimetres or so) – this will allow for a little shrinkage as it cooks and creates a nice neat finish. Chill in the fridge whilst you prepare the filling.

Slice the leeks into 1.5–2cm rounds – when stood up on their ends, you want the leeks to be just a little higher than the depth of your tartlet tins once they are lined with pastry.

Put the oil and butter into a frying pan and melt together over a low heat. Place the leeks, cut-sides down, in the pan, lining them up neatly so they fit snugly against one another. Tear off a sheet of greaseproof paper big enough to cover the pan, scrunch up and briefly rinse under running water. Shake off the excess water and then cover the leeks with the dampened paper, tucking the paper down the edges so that it sits within the frying pan. This creates a steamy lid that'll help the leeks soften without getting too hot. Leave the leeks to gently sweat for 8–10 minutes or until they are beginning to soften and take on just the smallest hint of colour. Uncover and use a table knife to help you turn the leeks over so that the top-sides are now facing down. Re-cover with the damp paper (dampening the paper again with a little more water, if necessary) and cook for a further 4–5 minutes or until they are soft but not collapsing. Remove from the heat and discard the paper, then set the leeks aside to cool slightly.

Preheat the oven to 200°C/180°C fan/gas 6 and place a heavy baking sheet on a shelf in the oven to heat up.

Remove the tartlet cases from the fridge. Again using a table knife to help, divide the leeks between the tartlet cases, with the cut-sides facing uppermost. Tuck in a little sprig or two of thyme to each tartlet.

In a jug, lightly beat the eggs and cream together, seasoning well with salt and freshly ground black pepper. Slowly pour into the pastry cases over the leeks, allowing it to flow into the gaps around the leeks. Top each tartlet with the cheese and season with another grind of black pepper.

Remove the hot baking sheet from the oven and carefully slide each tartlet onto it. Bake in the oven for about 25 minutes or until golden brown on top and the pastry is cooked through. Carefully remove the tartlets from the tins to serving plates and serve hot or warm. As a starter, these tartlets need no accompaniment. Add salad if you are serving these as more of a complete meal.

Wild Mushroom, Butter Bean and Sherry Pie

I have had a long love affair with sherry, both as a delicious drink and a versatile cooking ingredient, and as such, there is nearly always a bottle slotted into the prime door position in my fridge. Whilst enduringly popular in its native Spain, sherry in the UK has travelled a great distance in recent years. It's no longer the preserve of dusty old aunts and happily it's currently facing something of a trendsetters boom. My sherry of choice for this creamy vegetarian pie is something dark and rich but still dry – an Oloroso or Palo Cortado is ideal. Paler sherries – Manzanilla, for example – will get a little lost among the deep mushroomy flavours.

Serves 4 | Takes 20 minutes to make (plus cooling), 1 hour 10 minutes to cook

200ml boiling water
30g dried porcini
50g unsalted butter
1 tbsp olive oil
600g mixed fresh mushrooms, torn into bite-size pieces
1 leek, washed and finely chopped
2 cloves garlic, crushed
loose handful of fresh sage leaves, chopped
175ml rich dry sherry, such as Oloroso or Palo Cortado
300ml double cream
2 x 400g cans butter beans, drained and rinsed
plain flour, for dusting
1/2 pack (250g) ready-made puff pastry
salt and freshly ground black pepper
beaten egg, to glaze
sea salt flakes, for sprinkling

Measure the boiling water into a jug and stir through the porcini. Set aside to soak for 30 minutes.

Meanwhile, melt the butter with the oil in a large, deep frying pan set over a medium-low heat. Add the fresh mushrooms, leek, garlic and sage and season with a little salt and freshly ground black pepper. Fry gently for around 10 minutes or until the mushrooms have softened – at first they will seem to dry up, then suddenly they will release all their liquid, so keep cooking until they have reabsorbed their juices.

Pour in the sherry and add the dried porcini along with their soaking water (leaving the last little bit of soaking water behind as it may be gritty). Bring to a simmer and simmer steadily for 5 minutes to reduce a little. Add the cream and butter beans, bring back to a simmer and cook gently for a further 10 minutes or so until the mixture is rich and thickened. Taste to check the seasoning, adding a little more salt and black pepper, if necessary. Remove from the heat, transfer to a large pie dish and set aside to cool completely – a layer of cling film pressed snugly onto the surface will prevent a skin forming.

Once the filling is cold, preheat the oven to 220°C/200°C fan/gas 7.

Brush the rim of the pie dish with a little cold water. On a lightly floured work surface, roll out the pastry to a thickness of about 3mm, then using the rolling pin to help you, lay the pastry over the filling, pressing down firmly at the edges to seal. Trim the edges using a small sharp knife and make a slit or two in the top of the centre of the pie to let the steam escape. Brush all over with beaten egg and sprinkle over a few sea salt flakes.

Bake in the oven for around 40 minutes or until the pastry is crisp, golden and puffed up. Serve hot. This is a rich pie so I'd be tempted here to keep the side dishes to simple, but plentiful, steamed vegetables.

Caramelised Red Onion, Cream and Stilton Quiche

When cooked long and slow, red onions take on an incredible depth of flavour, and in this quiche they form a sweet dense layer underneath a rich and creamy custard. You can replace the Stilton with mature Cheddar if you are not a blue cheese lover.

Serves 4–6 | Takes 15 minutes to make (plus cooling), 1 hour 5 minutes to cook

50g unsalted butter
1 tbsp olive oil
4 large red onions, thinly sliced
couple of sprigs of fresh thyme
2 tbsp balsamic vinegar
1 deep 25cm blind-baked Shortcrust Pastry Tart Case (see pages 6–7)
4 eggs
300ml single cream
200g Stilton, crumbled
salt and freshly ground black pepper
handful of rocket leaves, to garnish

Melt the butter with the oil in a large, deep saucepan. Stir through the onions and thyme sprigs, then cook, uncovered, over a very low heat for at least 30 minutes or until they are really soft, stirring occasionally. Remove and discard the thyme stalks.

Pour in the balsamic vinegar, increase the heat a little and continue to cook, stirring constantly for a few minutes until you are left with a dark rich mass of caramelised onions. Remove from the heat and set aside to cool – the onions will be very hot indeed so let them cool down until they are cool enough to touch.

Once the onions are cool, preheat the oven to 200°C/180°C fan/gas 6.

Spoon the onion mixture into the pastry tart case and spread evenly. In a bowl, beat together the eggs and cream and season well with salt and freshly ground black pepper. Slowly pour into the pastry tart case, allowing it to settle and find its own level gradually around the filling, then sprinkle over the Stilton.

Bake in the oven for about 30 minutes or until the filling is just set and the cheese is melted. Carefully remove the quiche from the tin and transfer it to a serving plate or wooden board. Serve hot or warm, scattered with a generous handful of rocket. This is a very rich quiche, so a simple salad dressed with a sharp dressing will work nicely as an accompaniment.

Chestnut, Shallot and Mushroom Pie

Thanks to the wine and the mushrooms, this deliciously rich pie has a slight autumnal feel to it and it is the perfect dish to bake on a chilly evening. Chestnuts have a satisfyingly 'meaty' bite to them, adding a great texture to the vegetarian filling in this pie.

Serves 4 | Takes 20 minutes to make (plus cooling), 1 hour 10 minutes to cook

25g unsalted butter
1 tbsp olive oil
12 shallots, peeled and halved lengthways
250g chestnut mushrooms, cut into quarters
2 bay leaves
2 sprigs of fresh rosemary, leaves picked and roughly chopped
1 heaped tbsp plain flour, plus extra for dusting
200g cooked (shelled) chestnuts (vacuum-packed ones are ideal), halved
200ml red wine
300ml vegetable stock
2 tsp Dijon mustard
small bunch of fresh flat-leaf parsley, finely chopped
$\frac{1}{2}$ pack (250g) ready-made puff pastry
salt and freshly ground black pepper
beaten egg, to glaze

Melt the butter and oil in a deep frying pan (adding the oil helps to stop the butter burning), then add the shallots and fry over a medium heat for about 15 minutes or until they are starting to soften and are lightly browned at the edges, stirring every now and then. Reduce the heat, stir through the mushrooms, then add the bay leaves and rosemary and cook gently for a further 10 minutes or so until the mushrooms have softened. Remove and discard the bay leaves. Stir through the flour until it has combined with the buttery juices.

Add the chestnuts, then gradually add the wine and stock, stirring constantly to prevent any lumps forming. Season with a little salt and freshly ground black pepper. Bring to the boil, then reduce the heat to as low as possible and simmer, uncovered, for around 20 minutes or until the vegetables are cooked, stirring occasionally. Stir in the mustard and parsley, taste to check the seasoning, adding a little more salt and black pepper, if necessary, then transfer to a large baking dish and set aside to cool completely.

Once the filling is cold, preheat the oven to 220°C/200°C fan/gas 7.

On a lightly floured work surface, roll out the pastry to a thickness of about 3mm. Brush the rim of the dish with a little cold water, then lay the pastry over the filling, pressing down firmly at the edges to seal and crimping the edges if you like. Cut a cross in the top of the pie to let the steam out and brush with a little beaten egg to glaze.

Bake in the oven for about 25 minutes or until the pastry is crisp and golden. Serve hot. For me, this pie has quite a traditional feel to it, so I always serve it with a bowl of steaming mashed potato alongside.

Camembert and Herb Filo Parcel for Two

Whilst perhaps not the ideal pie for a first date, this I think, is a perfectly luxurious thing to feed your loved one. Oozing cheese surrounded by crisp buttery pastry, this is definitely a pie to share and get stuck into together, rather than try and portion it out onto plates.

Serves 2 | Takes 20 minutes to make, 25 minutes to cook

1/2 pack (125g) filo pastry (5 sheets)

1 banana shallot, very finely chopped

2 tbsp chopped fresh mixed herbs (thyme, oregano, marjoram and tarragon are all lovely)

1 whole Camembert cheese (about 250g), unwrapped (or removed from its box)

1 clove garlic, peeled and sliced

25–50g butter, melted

salt and freshly ground black pepper

sourdough bread, to serve

Preheat the oven to 200°C/180°C fan/gas 6.

Unroll the filo pastry sheets and lay them on a clean dry work surface (keeping them as a stack). Scatter half of the shallot and half of the herbs in a little pile in the centre. Place the whole Camembert cheese on top, pierce a few slits in the surface and then poke the slices of garlic down inside the cheese. Scatter over the rest of the shallot and herbs, then season with a little salt and freshly ground black pepper.

Brush a little melted butter over the uppermost sheet of filo around the cheese and then bring up the 4 corners of the pastry to meet in the centre of the cheese, scrunching it together as you go. Brush a little more melted butter on the next sheet down, and bring up the 4 corners as before, scrunching it again. Repeat with all the remaining sheets of filo, enclosing the cheese completely, then brush a little more melted butter all over the outside layer, taking care not to damage the top, which should be elaborately ruffled and quite tall by now. Carefully lift the pie into a baking dish.

Bake in the oven for around 25 minutes or until the pastry is deep golden and crisp. Serve hot, in the baking dish. Serve split open with crisp toasted sourdough (see below) to dunk into the hot molten cheese. A bowl of crisp green salad to eat afterwards will be a pleasing contrast to the richness of the cheese.

To make the crisp toasted sourdough, cut thin slices from a slightly stale loaf of sourdough, rub them all over with a bruised clove of garlic and drizzle over a little olive oil. Arrange on a baking sheet and bake alongside the Camembert pie. It'll take around 15 minutes to crisp up, so put it in the oven 10 minutes or so after the pie.

Borlotti Bean, Squash, Red Pepper and Chard Pie with Goat's Cheese

This rainbow-coloured pie is magnificent to look at and it's certainly fit for a vegetarian feast! It's a pretty simple pie to make, but if there is a trick to be shared, then it is to make sure each distinct layer is really well seasoned and has plenty to offer in the taste department. You can use spinach if you can't get hold of chard.

Serves 6 (generously) | Takes 25 minutes to make (plus cooling), 1³/₄ hours to cook

6 tbsp olive oil

50g unsalted butter

2 onions, finely sliced

400g bunch rainbow chard, washed, stalks trimmed and chopped into 3–4cm pieces, and leaves roughly torn

1 large butternut squash (about 1.4kg), halved, deseeded and cut into 1cm-thick slices (I leave the peel on for texture)

2 whole bulbs of garlic

3 red, orange or yellow peppers, deseeded and cut into 3cm pieces

2 tbsp capers, drained and chopped

bunch of fresh flat-leaf parsley, chopped

2–3 tbsp harissa paste

400g can borlotti beans, drained and rinsed

plain flour, for dusting

double batch of Shortcrust Pastry (see pages 6–7)

250g soft rindless goat's cheese, crumbled

salt and freshly ground black pepper

1 egg, beaten, to glaze

cumin seeds and sea salt flakes, for sprinkling

Pour a tablespoon or so of the oil into a large frying pan, add the butter and set over a low heat. Once the butter has melted, stir in the onions, then cook gently, uncovered, for around 30 minutes or until very soft and lightly coloured, stirring from time to time. Add the chopped chard stalks, then cover and cook gently for a further 10 minutes, before adding the torn chard leaves and packing them down into a snug layer. Cover and let the leaves steam and wilt for about 10 minutes. Remove from the heat, season to taste with salt and freshly ground black pepper, then set aside to cool completely.

Whilst the onion and chard mixture is cooking, roast the squash and peppers. Preheat the oven to 220°C/200°C fan/gas 7. Spread the squash out over 1 or 2 large roasting tins and drizzle over a little of the remaining oil. Season well with salt and black pepper and tuck in the garlic bulbs. Put the mixed peppers in another roasting tin and drizzle the remaining oil over them, along with a little grind of salt and black pepper. Put both vegetables in the oven to roast until cooked and lightly coloured in places, around 35–40 minutes. The squash may take a few minutes more than the

peppers, which is why they are cooked in separate tins. Remove from the oven and set aside to cool completely. Once cold, stir the capers and parsley through the peppers. Separate the garlic into cloves and squeeze the soft flesh onto the squash, leaving the cloves as whole as possible.

In a small bowl, stir the harissa paste through the borlotti beans and season with a grind of salt and black pepper. Cover and set aside at room temperature.

Once the vegetables are all cold, preheat the oven to 200°C/180°C fan/gas 6. Set a heavy baking sheet on a shelf in the oven to heat up. Grease and base-line a 23cm springform cake tin with non-stick baking paper and set aside.

On a lightly floured work surface, cut the pastry into two-thirds and one-third, rolling each piece gently into a ball as you do so. Roll out the larger piece into a rough circle, about 4mm thick (the pastry needs to be slightly thicker here as the filling is so robust it needs a sturdy crust to hold it in) and use it to line the prepared springform cake tin, bringing it up the sides of the tin and leaving a little excess hanging over the edge.

To construct the layers, start by adding half of the roast butternut squash in a neatly packed layer at the bottom of the pastry-lined tin. Follow this with the harissa-spiked borlotti beans, spreading them out evenly, then add the roast peppers in an even layer. Next, add the wilted chard and onions mixture in an even layer, followed by the other half of the squash, making sure you level each layer before you add the next. Finally, sprinkle over the goat's cheese evenly. By now your pie will be full to the brim!

Brush the rim of the pastry with a little cold water to dampen it. Roll out the smaller piece of pastry so it is slightly bigger than the top of the tin and about 4mm thick and lay it over the filling, pressing down firmly and rolling and crimping the edges to seal. Make a couple of slits in the top of the pie to let the steam out. Brush all over with beaten egg and sprinkle over a few cumin seeds and sea salt flakes.

Carefully slide the tin onto the hot baking sheet in the oven and bake for about 50–55 minutes or until the pastry is cooked through and deep golden brown.

Remove from the oven and leave to cool in the tin for 20 minutes before sliding a knife around the inside edge of the tin and releasing the springform. Carefully transfer the pie to a serving plate or wooden board. This is a solid pie – I find the best way to get it off the base is to lay a plate over the top of the pie and turn it over quickly so it is upside-down. Peel off the paper and base of the tin before covering with a serving plate and inverting it quickly so it's now the right way up. Serve hot (it keeps its temperature very well) or warm, cut into thick slices. This pie is packed full of veggies so doesn't really need anything to accompany it, but a big green leafy salad will add a nice bit of crunch.

Watercress and Brie Tart

I adore watercress both for its vibrant peppery flavour and the fact that it feels so darn healthy to eat. In this rich tart, you get plenty of the former but I'm afraid the health-giving properties are rather counteracted by the Brie and crème fraîche – but it is a truly delicious treat nevertheless.

Serves 4–6 | Takes 15 minutes to make, 55 minutes to cook

1 tbsp olive oil
25g unsalted butter
1 onion, finely chopped
1 clove garlic, crushed
150g watercress (2 bags), washed and well drained
a little freshly grated nutmeg
1 shallow 25cm blind-baked Shortcrust Pastry Tart Case (see pages 6–7)
4 eggs
300g crème fraîche
100g Brie, cubed
salt and freshly ground black pepper

Put the oil and butter into a large, deep frying pan and set over a low heat. Stir through the onion and cook gently, uncovered, for around 25 minutes or until soft and translucent. Add the garlic and watercress and a few gratings of nutmeg and cook over a low heat, stirring, until the watercress has wilted. Remove from the heat and set aside to cool slightly.

Preheat the oven to 200°C/180°C fan/gas 6.

Spoon the watercress mixture into the pastry tart case and spread evenly. In a bowl, lightly whisk the eggs and crème fraîche together, then season with salt and freshly ground black pepper. Slowly pour into the pastry tart case, allowing it to settle and find its own level gradually around the filling. Top with the cubes of Brie and grind over a final twist of black pepper.

Bake in the oven for around 30 minutes or until the filling is just set. Carefully remove the tart from the tin and place it on a serving plate or wooden board. Serve hot or warm with a large bowl of mixed salad leaves alongside. If you fancy some extra carbs, hot new potatoes tossed in butter and a little chopped fresh parsley are ideal.

Red Pepper Pie with Anchovies, Black Olives and Basil

This is a big generous pie packed full of Mediterranean flavours and it's perfect for casual summery entertaining. If you want to make this vegetarian, swap the anchovies for a couple of tablespoonfuls of roughly chopped capers.

Serves 6 (generously) | Takes 20 minutes to make (plus cooling), 1½ hours to cook

3 tbsp olive oil
4 large red peppers, deseeded and chopped
4 cloves garlic, crushed
3 x 400g cans chopped tomatoes
1 tsp granulated sugar
50g can anchovies, drained and roughly chopped
3 tbsp stoned (drained) black olives, roughly chopped
large handful of fresh basil leaves, roughly chopped
4 eggs, lightly beaten
plain flour, for dusting
double batch of Shortcrust Pastry (see pages 6–7)
200g ricotta cheese
salt and freshly ground black pepper

Heat the oil in a large saucepan until it is really hot. Add the peppers and fry over a high heat for around 15–20 minutes or until they start to caramelise at the edges, stirring every now and then. Be brave, a little colour, even slight charring here and there, will add loads of flavour giving the peppers an almost roasted taste.

Add the garlic and fry for just a few seconds before pouring in the tomatoes. Stir through the sugar and then reduce the heat a little. Bring to a simmer and simmer steadily, uncovered, for around 20 minutes or until the sauce has a thick and almost jam-like consistency, stirring occasionally.

Remove from the heat, stir through the anchovies, olives and basil and season to taste with salt and freshly ground back pepper. Leave to cool completely (spreading the mixture out on a shallow tray will considerably speed up the cooling process), before stirring through the beaten eggs.

Whilst the filling is cooling, prepare the pastry case. Preheat the oven to 200°C/180°C fan/gas 6.

On a lightly floured work surface, roll out the pastry to a thickness of about 3mm and use it to line a tin about 35 x 25cm in size – I use a shallow rectangular roasting tin lined with 2 wide strips of non-stick baking paper to help me lift the cooked pie out. Line the pastry case with non-stick baking paper and baking beans (see page 10 for more tips on blind-baking). Bake in the oven for 20 minutes. Remove the paper and beans, then bake for a further 5 minutes to cook the pastry through completely. Remove from the oven.

Spoon the red pepper mixture into the blind-baked pastry case, dot the ricotta cheese over the top, then grind a little extra black pepper over the cheese.

Bake in the oven for around 30–35 minutes or until the filling is just set. Remove from the oven and leave to cool slightly, then serve hot or warm in generous slices. This pie is lovely served with buttered new potatoes and a seasonal salad alongside.

Prawn and Smoked Salmon Tarts

There's no beating around the bush, these tarts are essentially large vol-au-vents, albeit knife and fork starter-size rather than retro canapé nibbles. And packed full of a delicious herby prawn and smoked salmon filling, these are about as far from retro as you can get. You can use a large fluted cutter for the classic vol-au-vent crinkly edge. I use the 12cm ring of an individual fluted tart tin.

Makes 4 individual tarts (ideal for a starter) | Takes 20 minutes to make (plus cooling), 20 minutes to cook

plain flour, for dusting
1 pack (500g) ready-made puff pastry
1 egg, beaten
4 tbsp crème fraîche
finely grated zest of 1 lemon, plus a squeeze of juice to taste
generous handful of chopped fresh herbs, such as dill, parsley and chives
250g cooked peeled prawns, well drained
125g smoked salmon, shredded into strips
salt and freshly ground black pepper
fresh dill sprigs, to garnish

Preheat the oven to 220°C/200°C fan/gas 7.

On a lightly floured work surface, roll out the pastry to form a large square about 3mm thick. Cut out 8 fluted circles, each about 12cm diameter. Lay 4 of these circles on a baking sheet and brush all over the tops with beaten egg. Take care not to brush egg down the cut edges of the pastry as this will stick the layers together and they won't puff up in the oven.

Take a round glass of about 10cm diameter and place in the centre of one of the remaining 4 circles and cut all around, removing the middle and leaving you with a 12cm ring of pastry. Discard the middle, or use to make another little snack (see page 12 for leftover pastry ideas). Repeat with the remaining 3 circles of pastry. Carefully lay the pastry rings over the egg-brushed circles, lining up the edges perfectly – these rings will puff up in the oven, creating the sides of the cases. Brush a little more beaten egg over the top of the rings, again taking care not to let the egg flow down over the edges. Bake in the oven for about 20 minutes or until puffed up and golden. Remove from the oven and set aside to cool completely.

To make the filling, mix the crème fraîche, lemon zest, a little lemon juice and the herbs together in a small bowl, seasoning well with salt and freshly ground black pepper. Stir through the prawns and most of the smoked salmon, reserving a little for the garnish.

Spoon the mixture into the cooked tart cases, dividing it evenly. Garnish with the extra smoked salmon and dill sprigs and serve immediately, as the pastry will lose its crispness over time. As a starter, these really need nothing to serve alongside, although you can scatter over a little peppery rocket, if you fancy.

Smoked Haddock and Creamed Spinach Pies

Smoked haddock goes so well with rich creamy sauces. I've paired it with creamed spinach to produce a rather luxurious fish pie. If you have one, use a salad spinner to dry the washed spinach really well. Wet spinach will result in a thin wet sauce rather than the thick creamy one you are aiming for.

Makes 4 individual pies | Takes 25 minutes to make (plus cooling), 1 hour 20 minutes to cook

1 tbsp olive oil
50g unsalted butter
2 onions, chopped
450g skinless smoked
    haddock fillets
2 bay leaves
1 clove garlic, crushed
700g fresh spinach, washed
    and drained very well, then
    roughly chopped
2 tbsp plain flour, plus extra
    for dusting
300ml milk
150ml double cream
freshly grated nutmeg, to
    taste
small bunch of fresh chives,
    snipped
double batch of Shortcrust
    Pastry (see pages 6–7)
salt and freshly ground black
    pepper
a little beaten egg or a
    mixture of milk and
    vegetable oil, to glaze

Put the olive oil and butter into a large saucepan and set over a low heat until melted. Stir through the onions and cook gently for around 20–25 minutes or until soft and translucent, stirring occasionally.

Meanwhile, arrange the smoked haddock fillets in a single layer in a large frying pan, cover with cold water, tuck in the bay leaves and grind over a little black pepper. Cover with a tight-fitting lid or piece of foil and bring to a simmer over a medium heat. Poach until the fish is just cooked through, around 10–15 minutes, depending on the thickness of the fillets. Remove from the heat and use a fish slice to remove the fish to a plate. Leave to cool for a few minutes before flaking the fish into bite-size pieces, then set aside. Discard the poaching water and bay leaves.

Once the onions are soft, add the garlic, stirring well to mix and then cook gently for 1 minute. Add the spinach, packing it well into the pan, then cover with a lid and let the spinach wilt down for a few minutes. If necessary, do this in 2 batches – the volume of leaves is alarming, but it will drastically reduce on wilting. Once all the spinach has been added and is wilted, sprinkle the flour thinly and evenly over the surface and stir well to mix.

Gradually pour in the milk, stirring continuously to blend in the flour smoothly, then bring to a simmer. Simmer steadily for about 5 minutes to cook the flour, then pour in the cream and season to taste with nutmeg and salt and black pepper. Finally, stir through the chives and flaked smoked haddock. Remove from the heat and set aside to cool completely – transferring the mixture to a shallow tray will speed this up considerably. A layer of cling film pressed onto the surface will also prevent a skin forming.

Once the filling is cold, preheat the oven to 200°C/180°C fan/gas 6 and place a heavy baking sheet on a shelf in the oven to heat up.

On a lightly floured work surface, cut the pastry into 2 pieces, making one piece slightly larger than the other. Cut the larger piece into 4 equal-size pieces, gently rolling each one into a ball. Roll out each ball to a thickness of about 3mm and use it to line an individual pie tin (each about 16 x 11cm), gently pressing down into the base and up the sides of the tin. Divide the filling evenly between the pie tins and brush the rims of the pastry with a little cold water. Cut the other piece of pastry into 4 equal-size pieces, then roll out each one as before to form the lids. Lay the lids over the pies, pressing down firmly at the edges to seal. Trim the edges with a small sharp knife, then crimp them if you like. Brush all over with a little beaten egg or a mixture of milk and oil, then cut a slit or two in the top of each pie to let the steam out.

Remove the hot baking sheet from the oven and carefully slide each pie onto it. Bake in the oven for around 35–40 minutes or until the pastry is cooked through and golden brown. Serve hot. Buttered new potatoes and carrots are lovely accompaniments for this pie.

Crab Quiche

This is a really rich and delicious quiche, and with all the cream and eggs and the expense of the crab meat, this is a dish best saved for a special treat. When I buy fresh crab meat, I always get a half and half mix of brown and white meat. The brown has absolutely bags of flavour and the white adds the 'crabby' texture. White crab meat alone will give you a rather more subtle seafood taste.

Serves 4–6 | Takes 15 minutes to make, 1 hour 5 minutes to cook

1 tbsp olive oil
25g unsalted butter
1 large red onion, finely chopped
300ml single cream
3 eggs
1 tbsp tomato purée
1 tsp paprika (unsmoked)
200g fresh crab meat (a mix of half brown and half white meat)
1 shallow 25cm blind-baked Shortcrust Pastry Tart Case (see pages 6–7)
salt and freshly ground black pepper

Put the oil and butter into a frying pan and set over a low heat. Once the butter has melted, stir through the onion and cook gently, uncovered, for 30 minutes or so until it is soft and very lightly caramelised, stirring occasionally. Remove from the heat and set aside to cool slightly.

Preheat the oven to 200°C/180°C fan/gas 6.

In a bowl, lightly beat the cream, eggs, tomato purée and paprika together. Add the crab meat and cooked onion, seasoning well with salt and freshly ground black pepper, and lightly mix together. Slowly pour into the pastry tart case.

Bake in the oven for around 35 minutes or until the filling is just set and golden brown. Carefully remove the quiche from the tin and place it on a serving plate or wooden board. Serve hot, warm or cold. New potatoes tossed in chopped fresh parsley and green salad are both great accompaniments.

Stargazy Pie with Sardines and Samphire

This pie originates from the small fishing community of Mousehole in Cornwall. It's an unusual and delicious dish where pilchards or sardines are baked under a pastry top along with eggs and potatoes. Traditionally, whole fish are used, with their heads and tails poking out of the pastry, and presented like this it certainly has lots of wow factor. However, it does make for slightly fiddly eating as you dissect the fish from the bones, but this enforced slowing down is probably a good thing – this is a pie to linger over! If all that rather puts you off, you can always get your fishmonger to fillet the fish for you and just use the heads and tails as a sort of 'garnish' to embellish. In my version, I have added samphire for a lovely seaside crunch – it's not the easiest vegetable to get hold of but a fishmonger is probably your best bet for tracking it down. Samphire can be a little salty, so give it a good rinse under cold running water before use. The smoked paprika sprinkled on top is hardly regional Cornish, but I love the colour it adds to the crisp crust.

Serves 4 | Takes 25 minutes to make (plus cooling), 1½ hours to cook

1 tbsp olive oil
25g unsalted butter
2 large onions, finely chopped
4 rashers streaky bacon, chopped
couple of sprigs of fresh lemon thyme
150ml Madeira (or white wine)
600g Charlotte potatoes (or other waxy salad potatoes), cut into 5mm-thick slices
350ml fish stock
100g samphire
4 eggs, hard-boiled, cooled and peeled
4 large fresh sardines, gutted, but left whole
plain flour, for dusting
½ pack (250g) ready-made puff pastry
freshly ground black pepper

To glaze
1 tbsp milk
1 tbsp olive oil
sea salt flakes

Spanish smoked paprika (optional)

Put the olive oil and butter into a deep frying pan and set over a low heat. Once the butter has melted, add the onions, bacon and lemon thyme sprigs and cook gently, uncovered, for around 30 minutes, stirring from time to time. You want the onions to soften to a sweetly melting base but not really colour, so be patient.

Add the Madeira, then turn up the heat and allow it to reduce for 5 minutes. Stir through the potato slices, coating them well in the juices and then pour in the stock. Bring to a steady simmer, cover with a lid and cook over a low heat for around 20–30 minutes or until the potatoes are tender but not collapsing. Stir from time to time to make sure the mixture cooks evenly, and remove the lid halfway through cooking if there is an excess of stock (most of the stock should be absorbed by the potatoes as they cook).

Remove from the heat, remove and discard the thyme stalks, then stir through the samphire and add some freshly ground black pepper to taste. Transfer the mixture to a suitable pie dish or tin – a rectangular one about 30 x 24cm is ideal as it will make portioning out the fish easier – and leave to cool completely.

Once the potato mixture is cold, preheat the oven to 220°C/200°C fan/gas 7.

Cut the hard-boiled eggs in half lengthways and arrange evenly over the potato mixture. Lay the sardines widthways like sleeping soldiers across the surface, alternating them head to tail.

Brush the rim of the pie dish with a little cold water. On a lightly floured work surface, roll out the pastry to a thickness of about 3mm and gently lift it over the pie filling, but don't press down just yet. This next part is a little fiddly, but using a small sharp knife, make a small incision through the pastry at the head and tail of each fish. With one hand under the pastry blanket and the other above, feed the heads and tails through the slits you have just made. Trim the pastry to fit the dish or tin and press down firmly at the edges to seal.

For the glaze, whisk the milk and oil together in a small bowl, then brush all over the surface of the pie. Sprinkle over some sea salt flakes and smoked paprika, if using, and then slide the pie into the hot oven. Bake for around 30 minutes or until the pastry is crisp and golden. Serve hot. This pie really has all you need within it, but a green salad or some seasonal green vegetables make a nice extra to serve alongside.

Chicken, White Wine and Tarragon Pie

This is a chicken pie to be made with only love and patience, the sort of thing I find best saved for a wet and windy afternoon when the kitchen feels like the nicest place to hang out. So, not a quick-fix pie by any means, but possibly the best, creamiest chicken pie you'll ever taste. Use the best quality chicken you can afford – the stock you get from a happy free-range or organic bird with plenty of space to roam and exercise will be far superior.

Serves 4–6 | Takes 25 minutes to make (plus cooling), 2 hours 50 minutes to cook

For the poached chicken
1 chicken (about 1.6–1.8kg)
3 carrots, unpeeled and cut into chunks
2 onions, unpeeled and cut into quarters
2 bay leaves
1/2 tsp whole black peppercorns

For the sauce
50g unsalted butter
1 tbsp olive oil
1 large onion, finely chopped
4 rashers smoked streaky bacon, chopped
1 clove garlic, crushed
250ml white wine
60g plain flour, plus extra for dusting
500ml chicken stock (from poaching the chicken)
150ml double cream
few sprigs of fresh tarragon, leaves picked and chopped
salt and freshly ground black pepper

double batch of Rough Puff Pastry (see pages 7–8)
beaten egg, to glaze
sea salt flakes, for sprinkling

For the poached chicken, put the whole chicken into a large stockpot and cover with cold water. Set over a medium heat and bring to the boil, adding the carrots, onions, bay leaves and peppercorns to the pot as it comes up to temperature. Reduce the heat to a minimum, then cover tightly and simmer very gently for about 1 hour or until the chicken is cooked.

Using a slotted spoon and a carving fork, remove the chicken to a plate, allowing the juices to drain back into the pot. Set the chicken aside to cool a little, then remove and discard the skin and bones and shred the meat into bite-size pieces. Set the meat aside to cool completely, then chill until needed.

Return the stock in the pot to the stove and turn the heat up a little, then simmer steadily, uncovered, for a further 45–55 minutes or until the stock is reduced by about half. Strain the stock through a colander into a bowl and discard the vegetables and herbs. Measure the liquid – you should be left with around 500ml stock. Make up with a splash of water if you are a little under, or discard the excess or save for another recipe if you are a little over.

Once the stock is about halfway through reducing, start the base of the sauce. Melt the butter with the oil in a large saucepan over a low heat. Add the onion and bacon and cook gently for around 20 minutes or so until the onion is soft and very lightly caramelised, stirring from time to time. Add the garlic and cook for another couple of minutes, before pouring in the wine. Bring to a simmer and simmer steadily for about 10 minutes or until the wine has nearly all reduced, then stir through the flour, mixing it well into the onion base.

Gradually pour in the stock, stirring all the time until the sauce has thickened, then simmer steadily for about 5 minutes to cook the flour. Add the cream and tarragon and season well with salt and freshly ground black pepper. Remove from the heat and set aside to cool completely – press a layer of cling film onto the surface to prevent a skin forming. Once cold, fold through the shredded chicken meat.

Once the filling is cold, preheat the oven to 220°C/200°C fan/gas 7 and set a heavy baking sheet on a shelf in the oven to heat up.

On a lightly floured work surface, cut the pastry into 2 pieces, making one piece slightly larger than the other. Roll out the larger piece to a thickness of about 3mm and use it to line a large pie tin (a rectangular roasting tin, about 30 x 25cm is ideal). Spoon the filling into the pastry case, levelling with a spoon. Brush the rim of the pastry with a little cold water. Roll out the other piece of pastry so it is slightly bigger than the top of the tin and lay it over the filling, pressing down well onto the bottom piece of pastry to seal the edges. Trim the edges with a small sharp knife and crimp them if you like, then cut a couple of slits in the top of the pie to let the steam out. Brush all over with beaten egg to glaze and sprinkle with a few sea salt flakes.

Slide the pie onto the hot baking sheet in the oven and bake for 45–50 minutes or until the pastry is deep golden brown and cooked through. Serve whilst piping hot and bubbling. Yet again, mashed potato is great served with this pie. As it is a little bit special, I might be tempted to up the ante and serve it with creamy celeriac mash as a treat instead.

Ox Cheek, Oyster and Stout Pies

I like to make these as individual pies. All beef pies deserve to be served with a good mash to soak up the rich gravy. Go the extra mile with a perfectly smooth pomme purée, laced with plenty of double cream and butter.

Makes 4 good-size individual pies | Takes 20 minutes to make (plus cooling), 2 hours 55 minutes to cook

2 tbsp plain flour, plus extra for dusting

800g ox cheek (or other beef cut suitable for a long, slow braise, such as skirt, shin or chuck steak), cut into bite-size pieces

2 tbsp olive oil

2 onions, 2 carrots and 2 sticks celery, all finely chopped

2 bay leaves

500ml Guinness or other stout

300ml beef stock

12 large fresh oysters (in shell)

about 2/3 pack (325g) ready-made puff pastry

salt and freshly ground black pepper

beaten egg, to glaze

sea salt flakes, for sprinkling

Put the flour into a bowl and season with salt and freshly ground black pepper. Toss the beef pieces in the seasoned flour to coat lightly all over. Pour the oil into a flameproof casserole and set over a high heat. When the oil is smoking hot, quickly sear the floured beef in batches until it's brown on all sides. Remove each batch to a plate using a slotted spoon, then brown the remaining beef. Once all the beef has been seared, reduce the heat to low.

Add the onions, carrots and celery and cook for about 10 minutes or until they start to soften a little. Return all the beef and any juices to the casserole and stir well. Tuck in the bay leaves and then pour over the Guinness and stock. Bring to a simmer, then cover with a lid and simmer gently, stirring from time to time, until the meat is really soft and tender – this will take anything from 1 1/2–2 hours.

Whilst the beef is cooking, shuck the oysters. Lay an oyster, flat-side uppermost, on a tea towel and grip it firmly using the towel. Carefully insert the point of an oyster knife (a stubby, stiff-bladed blunt knife) into the hinge end of the shell, wiggling it back and forth to prise the two halves open. Run the knife around the under-surface of the flat shell to separate the muscle neatly, then lift off the top shell. Run the knife underneath the oyster meat to release it from the bottom shell, tipping it and its liquor into a bowl, picking out any fragments of shell as you do so. Repeat with the remaining oysters and then chill until required. Discard the oyster shells or use them to make a pleasing decoration – after testing this pie, I piled the cleaned shells up as a little sculpture on one corner of a raised bed in my garden.

Once the beef is tender, remove it from the casserole with a slotted spoon and divide it between 4 individual pie dishes. Set these aside. Turn the heat up and reduce the sauce in the casserole to a desired consistency – I like mine quite thick. Adjust the seasoning to taste, adding a little more black pepper, if you like. If the sauce needs more salt, pour in a little of the reserved oyster liquor (but don't add the oysters yet), then pour the sauce over the meat. Leave to cool completely, and then once cold, top each portion of the meat with 3 oysters, pressing them lightly into the sauce.

Once the filling is cold, preheat the oven to 220°C/200°C fan/gas 7.

On a lightly floured work surface, cut the pastry into 4 equal-size squares. Roll out each square to fit your pie dishes, rolling them slightly larger so you can trim the edges to fit. Brush the rims of the pie dishes with a little cold water, then lay a piece of pastry over the filling in each dish, pressing down firmly at the edges to seal. Trim the edges with a small sharp knife, then cut a slit in the top of each pie to let the steam out. Brush the pastry with a little beaten egg and sprinkle over a few sea salt flakes.

Bake in the oven for around 25–30 minutes or until the pastry is crisp, puffed up and golden brown. Serve hot. These are posh pies, and as such, I recommend serving them with posh mash! Exquisitely smooth pomme purée or creamy celeriac purée are my choices.

Venison Pie with Port and Redcurrant Jelly

A deeply autumnal pie if ever there was one, the sort of thing to fuel your body and cheer your mind at that point in the year when the onset of winter is inevitable. Venison is a wonderful meat that I'd like to see being easier to get hold of, and with the rules of supply and demand, the more we buy the more readily available it will become. It's naturally free-range, low in fat, high in iron and truly delicious to boot.

Serves 4–6 | Takes 20 minutes to make (plus cooling), 3 hours 10 minutes to cook

- 2 tbsp plain flour, plus extra for dusting
- 1.2kg venison shoulder or neck, trimmed and cut into bite-size pieces
- 3 tbsp olive oil
- 6 rashers smoked streaky bacon, diced
- 12 shallots, peeled and left whole
- 3 cloves garlic, crushed
- a couple of sprigs of fresh thyme
- 900ml beef stock
- 200ml port
- 3 tbsp redcurrant jelly
- 1 batch of Rough Puff Pastry (see pages 7–8) or use 1 pack (500g) ready-made puff pastry, if you prefer
- salt and freshly ground black pepper
- 1 egg, beaten, to glaze
- sea salt flakes, for sprinkling

Sprinkle the flour into a mixing bowl and season with a little salt and freshly ground black pepper. Add the venison and toss well to evenly coat each piece in a little flour. Pour about half of the oil into a heavy-based flameproof casserole and set over a high heat. When the oil is really hot, brown the venison pieces in batches, a handful at a time, until they are nicely browned all over. Remove each batch to a plate and continue until all the venison is browned, adding a splash more oil, if necessary.

Reduce the heat a little, add the bacon and shallots to the casserole and fry for around 10 minutes or until they are starting to colour a little at the edges, stirring occasionally. Stir through the garlic and then add all the meat plus any juices back to the casserole. Tuck in the thyme sprigs and then pour in the stock and port. Bring to the boil, then reduce the heat to as low as possible, cover and simmer gently until the meat is really tender – this can take between 1¹⁄₂–2 hours, just keep checking and stirring occasionally. Once the meat is ready, use a slotted spoon to remove the venison to a large baking dish and set aside.

Turn the heat up a little, stir through the redcurrant jelly and then simmer the sauce to a desired consistency – the time for this may vary depending on how long the venison was cooking for, but you want the sauce to coat the back of a wooden spoon. Once you are happy, taste it and add a little more salt and black pepper if necessary, then fish out and discard the thyme stalks. Pour the sauce over the meat, then set aside to cool completely.

Once the filling is cold, preheat the oven to 220°C/200°C fan/gas 7.

On a lightly floured work surface, roll out the pastry to fit the top of your baking dish, aiming for a thickness of about 3mm. Depending on the shape of your chosen dish, you may have more pastry than you need (see page 12 for ideas on how to use leftover pastry). Brush the rim of the dish with a little cold water, then lay the pastry over the filling, pressing down firmly at the edges to seal. Trim the edges with a small sharp knife, then crimp them if you like. Cut a couple of slits in the top of the pie to let the steam out, then brush the surface with beaten egg and sprinkle over a few sea salt flakes.

Bake in the oven for around 40 minutes or until the pastry is crisp and golden and the filling is bubbling hot. Serve hot. This pie is wonderful served with creamy mashed potato and a bowl of braised red cabbage.

Greek Lamb Filo Pie with Feta and Oregano

This pie is a triumph of rich Mediterranean flavours – a rich ragù sauce topped with herb and garlic-laced feta cheese and baked with a crisp lid of filo pastry. It's the perfect al fresco meal for sharing with friends on a sunny evening. The long slow cooking of the lamb is important as it enriches and gathers much flavour over time. Although it takes a while to cook, this is a very straightforward pie to make, with no making or rolling of pastry, so it's perfect for stress-free yet impressive entertaining.

Serves 4–6 | Takes 25 minutes to make (plus cooling), 2 hours 10 minutes to cook

- 1 tbsp olive oil
- 800g minced lamb
- 2 large onions, chopped
- 4 large cloves garlic, crushed
- 1 heaped tsp ground allspice
- 1 heaped tsp ground cinnamon
- a pinch of dried mixed herbs
- a pinch of dried chilli flakes (optional)
- 400g ripe cherry tomatoes, halved
- 400ml lamb or beef stock
- 250ml white wine
- 300g feta cheese, crumbled
- generous bunch of fresh oregano, leaves picked and roughly chopped
- 2 cloves garlic, finely chopped
- finely grated zest of 1 lemon
- 1 pack (250g) filo pastry (there are about 10 sheets in a pack but you won't need them all – you only need 5 or 6, so use the rest in another recipe or freeze them)
- a little olive oil, for brushing
- salt and freshly ground black pepper
- sea salt flakes, for sprinkling

Pour the oil into a large, deep frying pan and set over a high heat. Add the mince, breaking it up with a wooden spoon, and fry for around 15 minutes or until nicely browned. Don't stir too much as you want the meat to catch and stick in places – this caramelisation will add lots of intense flavour to the finished dish.

Reduce the heat a little and stir through the onions, then fry for a further 10 minutes or so until the onions are starting to soften and turn translucent. Add the crushed garlic, the allspice, cinnamon, dried herbs and chilli flakes, if using, and fry for just another minute or so before adding the tomatoes, stock and wine. Season with salt and freshly ground black pepper. Bring to the boil, then reduce the heat to as low as possible and simmer, uncovered, for around 1 hour or until the sauce is thick and rich, stirring occasionally. Taste to check the seasoning, adding a little more salt and black pepper, if necessary, then transfer to a large baking dish and leave to cool completely.

Once the filling is cold, preheat the oven to 200°C/180°C fan/gas 6.

In a small mixing bowl, stir together the feta, oregano, finely chopped garlic and the lemon zest, then sprinkle it evenly over the meat mixture. Unroll a sheet of filo pastry onto the work surface, then cover the rest with a clean damp tea towel to keep it supple. Brush the filo sheet with a little oil, then lay it over the filling, crumpling it in little waves over the surface. Brush another sheet of filo with oil and lay it over the first sheet, crumpling it as before, then repeat until you have around 5 or 6 layers (placed on top of each other) that completely cover the filling. Sprinkle lightly with sea salt flakes, along with a last drizzle of oil over the top layer.

Bake in the oven for around 35–40 minutes or until the pastry is crisp and deep golden brown. Serve hot. This pie is complete when served with a Greek-style salad of super ripe tomatoes, black olives, cucumber, green pepper and red onion, dressed in lemon juice and olive oil – sunshine in a bowl.

Steak and Portobello Mushroom Suet Pudding

This is my version of the hearty winter classic, steak and kidney pudding, which to my mind definitely falls into the pie category. I have to admit I feel no love whatsoever for kidneys, so here I have swapped them for thick slices of meaty Portobello mushrooms. This dish does take plenty of time to cook, but as most of it is entirely hands-off, it's a nice thing to do on a wet and windy afternoon when a warm steamy kitchen is the most appealing place to be.

Serves 4 | Takes 30 minutes to make (plus cooling), 4 hours 20 minutes to cook

For the filling

2 tbsp plain flour, plus extra for dusting
500g skirt beef, sliced into 1cm strips across the grain
2–3 tbsp olive oil
2 onions, chopped
5 large Portobello mushrooms (about 5), sliced into 1cm strips
300ml beef stock
200ml red wine
small bunch of fresh sage, leaves picked and chopped
salt and freshly ground black pepper

For the suet crust pastry

a little butter, for greasing
300g self-raising flour
150g shredded beef or vegetable suet
$^{1}/_{2}$ tsp fine salt
12–13 tbsp ice-cold water

To make the filling, sprinkle the flour into a mixing bowl and season with a little salt and freshly ground black pepper. Add the beef and toss well to evenly coat each strip in a little flour. Pour a little oil into a heavy-based flameproof casserole and set over a high heat. When the oil is really hot, brown the meat strips in batches, a handful at a time, until they are nicely caramelised in places. Remove each batch to a plate and continue until all the beef is browned, adding a splash more oil, if necessary.

Reduce the heat a little, then add the onions and fry for around 10 minutes or until they are just starting to soften, stirring occasionally. Return all the beef to the casserole, along with any juices, and then stir through the mushrooms. Pour in the stock and wine and stir through the sage, then bring gently to the boil. Turn the heat down to a minimum, cover with a lid or snug-fitting piece of foil and simmer very gently for around $1^{1}/_{2}$–2 hours or until the meat is meltingly tender and the sauce is well reduced, stirring once or twice. Remove the lid about halfway through cooking to allow the sauce to thicken.

Taste to check the seasoning, adding a little more salt and black pepper, if necessary. Remove from the heat and set aside to cool completely – spreading the mixture out in a shallow dish will speed this up considerably.

Once the filling is almost cold, make the suet crust pastry. First, grease a 1.2 litre pudding basin well with butter and set aside. In a large mixing bowl, mix the flour, suet and salt together until evenly mixed. Add the ice-cold water, a spoonful at a time, until the dough comes together in a rough ball with very little loose flour left. Suet crust pastry takes a lot more water than regular shortcrust pastry so keep trickling in as much as you need. Use your hands to bring it together into a ball, mopping up any excess flour as you do so, and then tip it onto the work surface. Knead gently for a couple of minutes until smooth and quite elastic.

Lightly dust the work surface with a little more flour and roll out the pastry to a thickness of about 5mm. Use it to line the prepared pudding basin, pressing the pastry well into the bottom and up the sides of the basin, then trim off most of the excess around the rim, leaving a 1cm overhang.

Spoon the filling into the pastry-lined basin, packing it down well and leaving behind any extra sauce that doesn't fit in. To make the pastry lid, re-roll the pastry trimmings to form a 5mm-thick circle that is a little larger than the top of the bowl. Brush a little cold water on the top edges of the pastry in the basin, gently lay the pastry circle over the filling, then fold the overhanging pastry over the edges of the pastry lid. Press down firmly all around the edges to seal the top lid to the sides.

Cover the top of the basin with a piece of non-stick baking paper, securing it tightly with string, then cover this with a snug-fitting piece of foil. Lower the pudding into a large saucepan, resting the bottom on an upturned saucer to keep it from directly touching the heat. Pour enough boiling water into the pan so that it comes about halfway up the sides of the basin. Bring to a steady simmer. Cover tightly with a lid and steam for 2 hours, checking the water level once or twice and topping it up, if necessary.

Remove from the heat and carefully remove the basin from the pan. Unwrap and slide a blunt knife around the inside edge of the basin to loosen the pudding, then carefully invert it onto a serving plate. Serve immediately whilst piping hot. A big dish of buttered cabbage is a very good thing to eat alongside this pudding, and perhaps some potatoes, boiled or mashed, if you are feeling extra hungry.

Steak, Mushroom and Cannellini Bean Pies with Parmesan Pastry

These rich and quite decadent-tasting pies are great for feeding a crowd when you're feeling the pinch. A cheap but delicious cut of beef is bulked out with plenty of mushrooms and some hearty beans: luxurious without breaking the bank. This recipe serves 4, but is easily doubled or even trebled. Make sure you get the pan really really hot before adding the strips of meat, just a handful at a time, to sear them. The caramelisation of the outside will add much intensity to the flavour of the finished pies.

Makes 4 individual pies | Takes 20 minutes to make (plus cooling), 2 hours to cook

- **450g skirt steak**
- **3 tbsp olive oil**
- **2 onions, sliced**
- **3 cloves garlic, crushed**
- **350g Portobello mushrooms, sliced**
- **400g can cannellini beans, drained and rinsed**
- **loose handful of fresh sage leaves, chopped**
- **1 tbsp plain flour, plus extra for dusting**
- **350ml beef stock**
- **small glass of red wine (about 175ml)**
- **2 tbsp balsamic vinegar**
- **150ml double cream**
- **1 batch of Parmesan and Sage Rough Puff Pastry (see pages 7–8)**
- **salt and freshly ground black pepper**
- **sea salt flakes, for sprinkling**

Slice the skirt steak into 1cm-thick strips, making sure you cut across the grain for maximum tenderness. Heat the oil in a flameproof casserole set over a high heat until it is smoking hot and then quickly sear the beef strips in the oil, a handful at a time, to caramelise the outside. Transfer the beef to a plate and continue until all the meat has been seared.

Turn the heat down a little, then add the onions to the casserole and fry for 10 minutes or so until they are starting to soften and caramelise a little at the edges. Add the garlic and fry for just a minute or so more, before stirring through the mushrooms, cannellini beans and sage. Sprinkle over the flour, stirring well, and then gradually pour in the stock, wine and balsamic vinegar, stirring all the time to prevent any lumps forming. Add the meat back to the pan, along with any juices and season well with salt and freshly ground black pepper. Bring to the boil, then reduce the heat to a minimum, cover with a lid or snug-fitting piece of foil and simmer very gently for around 1 hour or until the meat is very tender, stirring every now and then.

Remove the lid and pour in the cream, reserving a couple of teaspoons to glaze the pastry. Simmer, uncovered, for a further 10–15 minutes or until the sauce has reduced a little. Remove from the heat, divide the beef mixture between 4 individual pie dishes and set aside to cool completely.

Once the beef mixture is cold, preheat the oven to 220°C/200°C fan/gas 7.

Lightly dust some flour over the work surface, then cut the pastry into 4 equal-size pieces. Roll out each piece to fit the top of the pie dish, brush the rims of the dishes with a little cold water, then lay a piece of pastry over the filling in each dish, pressing down firmly at the edges to seal and crimping the edges as you go. Mix 1 teaspoon cold water with the reserved cream and brush over the tops of the pies. Use a small sharp knife to cut a hole in the top of each pie to let the steam escape, then sprinkle over a few sea salt flakes.

Bake in the oven for about 25 minutes or until the pastry is puffed up and golden. Serve hot. As these pies have cannellini beans in them, you don't really need the extra carbohydrates that mashed potato provides, but it will be a nice treat nevertheless. A dish of something green will be very welcome too, such as green beans or broccoli.

Rabbit Pie with White Wine and Crème Fraîche

This recipe requires a rabbit to be jointed. The butcher will do it for you, but the cave girl in me rather enjoys it, and it's really not that hard to do. For this pie, you first cook the meat on the bone because this adds much in the flavour department, and then once the meat is tender, it gets stripped off the bone before baking it in the pie.

Serves 6–8 | Takes 25 minutes to make (plus cooling), 2 hours 20 minutes to cook

- 2 tbsp plain flour, plus extra for dusting
- 2 large skinned rabbits, each jointed into 6 pieces
- 3 tbsp olive oil
- 6 rashers smoked streaky bacon, chopped
- 4 large leeks, washed and sliced
- 3 sticks celery, finely diced
- 2 large carrots, finely diced
- 3 cloves garlic, crushed
- 500ml white wine
- 300ml chicken stock
- 2 tbsp Dijon mustard
- a couple of sprigs of fresh sage, leaves picked and chopped
- 2 heaped tsp cornflour
- 300g crème fraîche
- a squeeze of lemon juice, or to taste
- 1 batch of Rough Puff Pastry (see pages 7–8) or use 1 pack (500g) ready-made puff pastry, if you prefer
- salt and freshly ground black pepper
- 1 egg, beaten, to glaze
- sea salt flakes, for sprinkling

In a small bowl, season the flour with a little salt and freshly ground black pepper. Lay the rabbit pieces on a plate and dust all over with the seasoned flour. Heat the oil in a large, heavy-based flameproof casserole set over a high heat and fry the rabbit pieces in batches until nicely browned all over. Don't rush this step or overcrowd the casserole – this caramelisation will add much to the flavour. Remove all the fried rabbit pieces to a plate and set aside.

Return the casserole to the heat, reduce the heat and then add the bacon, leeks, celery, carrots and garlic and fry for 10 minutes, stirring occasionally. Pour in the wine and stock, stir through the mustard and sage, then return the rabbit pieces to the casserole, pressing them under the liquid as much as possible. Cover with a lid or snug-fitting piece of foil, then bring gently to the boil and simmer over a low heat for around 1 hour–1 hour 10 minutes or until the rabbit is really tender and starting to fall away from the bones. Remove from the heat. Using a slotted spoon, remove the rabbit pieces to a plate and leave to cool a little before shredding all the meat from the bones. Set the meat aside and discard the bones. Leave the vegetables and stock in the casserole and return it to the heat.

Measure the cornflour into a small bowl and add a tablespoon or so of the crème fraîche, mixing well to form a smooth paste. Stir in the rest of the crème fraîche, then add it to the casserole, stirring well over a medium-low heat for 5 minutes or so until slightly thickened. Remove from the heat, return the rabbit meat to the casserole and taste to check the seasoning, adding lemon juice to taste and a little more salt and black pepper, if necessary. Transfer the mixture to a large baking dish and leave to cool completely – a layer of cling film pressed onto the surface will prevent a skin forming.

Once the rabbit filling is cold, preheat the oven to 220°C/200°C fan/gas 7.

Dust the work surface with a little flour and roll out the pastry to fit the top of your pie dish, aiming for a thickness of about 3mm. Brush the rim of the pie dish with a little cold water and lay the pastry over the filling, pressing down firmly at the edges to seal. Trim the edges with a small sharp knife, then crimp them if you like. Make a couple of slits in the top of the pie to allow the steam to escape, then brush with a little beaten egg and sprinkle over a few sea salt flakes.

Bake in the oven for around 40 minutes or until the pastry is cooked, crisp and golden. Serve bubbling hot with a selection of your favourite veg and a bowl of buttery mash.

GAME

Raised Game Pie

This is a Christmas buffet table classic. Made the 'proper' way it does take rather a long time, but in my version, I've aimed to lessen the hassle somewhat. Many butchers sell diced mixed game meat ready-prepared, and instead of lengthy bone-boiling, I've opted for a couple of leaves of gelatine dissolved in hot stock and Madeira to make a tasty jelly. A note on the shape of tin to use to make the raised game pie: as with all bottom crust pies, a metal tin is ideal here to achieve the best crust. I use a small enamel basin with a flat bottom that is 14cm in diameter and 8cm deep. A small cake tin of similar dimensions makes a good alternative too, or failing that, a small loaf tin will make a lovely rectangular pie.

Serves 6 | Takes 40 minutes to make (plus chilling, cooling and overnight chilling), 1¹/₂ hours to cook

For the filling
500g prepared boneless mixed game meat (I use a mix of pheasant, partridge and rabbit), cut into 1–2cm cubes
200g smoked streaky bacon, diced
150ml Madeira
2 tbsp mustard seeds
2 tsp ground allspice
2 bay leaves, finely chopped
salt and freshly ground black pepper

1 batch of Hot Water Crust Pastry (see page 8)

For the jelly
2 leaves of gelatine
1 ham stock cube
150ml boiling water
50ml Madeira

To make the filling, put the game meat and bacon into a mixing bowl and then stir through the Madeira, mustard seeds, allspice, bay leaves and a generous seasoning of salt and freshly ground black pepper. Cover and leave to marinate for 2 hours in the fridge, or even better, leave it overnight.

Once the meat has marinated, make the pastry (see page 8), then wrap, shape and chill it in the fridge for 30–45 minutes to firm up, as directed.

Preheat the oven to 180°C/160°C fan/gas 4, and place a heavy baking sheet on a shelf in the oven to heat up.

Cut 2 long strips of double-thickness non-stick baking paper and use it to line your tin (see note on shape of tin to use in recipe introduction) in a cross shape, with the 4 tails hanging over the edge – this will really help you get the pie out of the tin after baking. Line the prepared tin with the chilled pastry and shape the pastry lid disc as directed in the Traditional Pork Pie recipe on page 34.

Pack the meat filling into the pastry-lined tin, pressing quite firmly so that it fills all the gaps, then top with the remaining flat pastry disc for the lid. Fold the overhanging pastry over the edges of the flat pastry disc on top, crimping all around the edges to seal. Pierce the top in the centre, twisting the knife to make a generous hole of about 5mm. Slide the pie onto the hot baking sheet in the oven and bake for about 1¹/₂ hours or until the pastry is crisp and golden brown. Remove from the oven and leave the pie to cool to room temperature in the tin.

Once the pie is cool, take a skewer and insert it into the hole in the top, piercing down through the meat and giving it a little wiggle to widen the hole.

To make the jelly, soak the gelatine sheets in cold water for 10 minutes to soften, then gently squeeze out the excess water. Crumble the stock cube into a jug and pour over the boiling water, then add the soaked gelatine, stirring until dissolved. Stir in the Madeira, then set aside to cool to room temperature. Slowly pour this liquid into the hole in the top of the cooled pie – a funnel will help this considerably. You may not need all of the liquid, just fill it up as much as you can. Transfer the pie to the fridge and chill overnight.

When you are ready to serve, use the paper tails to help lift the pie out of the tin, sliding a table knife around to ease the pie away from the edges of the tin if it is a little stuck. Serve cold in generous wedges with some sort of tangy chutney, or I rather like it served with a sharp homemade cranberry sauce.

A PIE IN THE HAND

There is something very lovely about being offered your own individual pie to eat. But it is also a thing of great convenience, perfect for eating on the go, for picnics or parties and for snacking. Culinary traditions the world over embrace the idea of something delicious wrapped in pastry, and in this chapter you will find pie recipes from all corners of the globe, as well as more familiar ones too. From tempting pasties and patties to tasty turnovers and tartlets, there is something for everyone.

Borlotti Bean, Aubergine and Tomato Filo Tartlets

The filling for these crisp tartlets is based on a Turkish meze dish called 'pilaki' – a delicious cold bean and tomato salad laced with plenty of garlic and extra virgin olive oil. Here, I've used the pilaki as a filling for crisp filo shells, turning it into great no-fork tartlets that are ideal for party eating. You can bake your filo cases and make the salad dressing well in advance – just don't fill the tartlet cases until you are ready to serve, as the pastry will turn from crisp to soggy within an hour or so.

Makes 10 individual tartlets | Takes 25 minutes to make (plus cooling), 1$\frac{1}{2}$ hours to cook

For the pilaki filling
3 tbsp olive oil
1 large onion, finely chopped
1 large aubergine, cut into 1cm cubes
3 cloves garlic, crushed
250g ripe cherry tomatoes, quartered
1 tbsp tomato purée
1 tsp granulated sugar
400g can borlotti beans, drained and rinsed
salt and freshly ground black pepper

For the tartlet cases
1 pack (250g) filo pastry (about 10 sheets)
50–75g butter, melted

To dress
3 tbsp extra virgin olive oil
juice of $\frac{1}{2}$ lemon, or to taste
small bunch of fresh flat-leaf parsley, roughly chopped

For the pilaki filling, heat the olive oil in a deep frying pan over a medium heat, add the onion and fry for 10–15 minutes or until starting to soften and lightly caramelise, stirring every now and then. Add the aubergine, then reduce the heat a little and continue to fry for a further 15 minutes or so until the aubergine is starting to soften and colour in places, stirring frequently.

Add the garlic and fry for a further minute, before adding the tomatoes, tomato purée, sugar and 400ml cold water. Season with a little salt and freshly ground black pepper. Bring to the boil, then reduce the heat to a steady simmer and simmer, uncovered, for about 30 minutes or until the sauce is thick and rich, stirring occasionally. Add the borlotti beans, bring back to a steady simmer and simmer for a further 10 minutes. Remove from the heat and leave to cool to room temperature.

Whilst the pilaki mixture is cooling, make the tartlet cases. Preheat the oven to 200°C/180°C fan/gas 6.

Unroll the stack of filo pastry sheets onto the work surface, then cut all the way through the stack into quarters, so each sheet will give you 4 small square-ish shapes. Keep the filo pastry pieces covered with a clean damp tea towel to keep them supple. Take a 12-hole muffin tin and brush a little melted butter in 10 of the holes. Press a piece of filo into one of the holes, allowing the edges to stick up over the top, then brush with a little more melted butter. Press another piece of filo on top of the first one and brush with more melted butter. Continue to build up the layers with 2 more pieces of filo and melted butter, creating 4 layers in the hole to make a filo case. Repeat with the remaining filo pieces and melted butter, assembling them in the remaining buttered holes, to make 10 filo cases in total.

Bake in the oven for around 15–20 minutes or until crisp and golden. Remove from the oven and leave to cool completely in the tin, before carefully easing the pastry cases from the tin using a table knife to help.

Once the pilaki mixture is cool, dress it with the extra virgin olive oil and lemon juice to taste. Stir through the parsley, then taste and add a little more salt and black pepper, if necessary.

When you are ready to serve, spoon the pilaki mixture into the pastry cases, dividing it evenly. Serve immediately. These tartlets are best served on their own and they make perfect party food.

Tenderstem Broccoli and Cambazola Tarts

These are perhaps the simplest pies in the entire book, but they are no less for that. They are created from less than a handful of ingredients and are ready in minutes. Tenderstem broccoli is a great ingredient that cooks really quickly, so it's just fab for speedy yet impressive dishes like this.

Makes 4 individual tarts | Takes 15 minutes to make (plus cooling), 15 minutes to cook

200g tenderstem broccoli, ends trimmed
1 pack (320g) really-rolled puff pastry (1 rectangular sheet)
200g Cambazola cheese (blue Brie), cut into thin slices
salt and freshly ground black pepper

Blanch the tenderstem broccoli in a pan of boiling water for 1 minute. Drain well, then plunge into cold water to stop the cooking process. Drain well again and set aside to cool completely.

Preheat the oven to 220°C/200°C fan/gas 7.

Unroll the pastry onto the work surface and cut it into 4 rectangular pieces, trimming the edges neatly with a sharp knife – a straight edge on puff pastry helps the layers to separate and allows it to puff up in the oven. Arrange on 2 baking sheets, leaving plenty of space around each one. Using the tip of a sharp knife, score a shallow line about 1cm in from the edge all the way around the edge of each piece of pastry, to create a border – this will help the pastry to puff up at the edges.

Top the pastry rectangles with the cooled tenderstem broccoli, arranging it nose-to-tail over the pastry. Lay the cheese slices over the top, making sure they cover the delicate broccoli tips to prevent them scorching in the oven. Season with a little salt and a grind of black pepper.

Bake in the oven for about 12–15 minutes or until the pastry is crisp and cooked through. Serve hot or warm with a punchy rocket and herb salad.

Curried Chickpea Samosas with Coriander Chutney

Indian samosas are traditionally made with samosa pastry, which needs to be deep-fried, but my take on these are made with filo pastry, which can be baked to be a bit more healthy. You can vary the amount of spice and chilli to suit your taste – I always veer towards hot!

Makes 10 samosas | Takes 25 minutes to make (plus cooling), 55 minutes to cook

For the coriander chutney
40g fresh coriander (a small bunch)
1 clove garlic, chopped
3 fresh green chillies, deseeded, if you prefer (or use less if you don't like too much heat)
1 tbsp caster sugar, or to taste
1 tsp salt, or to taste
juice of $1/_2$ lemon, or to taste

For the samosas
$1/_2$ medium butternut squash (about 500g), deseeded and chopped into 1cm cubes (I leave the peel on for texture)
bunch of spring onions, finely chopped
2 cloves garlic, chopped
2–3 tbsp curry paste (use whichever is your favourite)
2 fresh red chillies, finely chopped (deseeded, if you prefer)
2 tbsp vegetable oil
400g can chickpeas, drained and rinsed
bunch of fresh coriander, chopped
50g frozen peas
juice of $1/_2$ lemon, or to taste
1 pack (250g) filo pastry (about 10 sheets)

50g butter, melted, or vegetable oil
salt and freshly ground black pepper

First, make the coriander chutney. Place all the ingredients for the chutney into a food processor (or place them in a jug and use a hand-held stick blender) and purée until smooth. Taste and then add extra sugar, salt and lemon juice to your taste. Transfer to a bowl, cover and set aside at room temperature to allow the flavours to mingle, whilst you make the samosas.

Preheat the oven to 220°C/200°C fan/gas 7.

For the samosas, put the squash, spring onions and garlic into a roasting tin, stir through the curry paste, red chillies and oil, then season with a little salt and freshly ground black pepper. Roast in the oven for 30 minutes. Stir through the chickpeas and return to the oven for a further 10 minutes.

Remove from the oven and gently mash the squash mixture in the tin with a potato masher – it doesn't need to be smooth, lumpy is fine. Stir through the chopped coriander, the frozen peas (you don't have to defrost them first) and lemon juice to taste. Set aside to cool completely.

Once the vegetable mixture is cold, preheat the oven again to 220°C/200°C fan/gas 7.

Unroll the stack of filo pastry sheets onto the work surface, then cut lengthways all the way through the middle of the stack so that you have 20 strips, each about 10cm wide (this will vary a little depending on the size of your sheets). Keep the filo pastry strips covered with a clean damp tea towel to keep them supple. Take 1 strip of filo, brush with melted butter and then lay another strip of filo directly on top. Place a tablespoonful of the squash filling at one end of the layered filo strips and fold over the bottom left corner of the filo so you have a triangle shape. Continue to fold the filo up along the length of the pastry (enclosing the filling completely), continuing to make a triangle shape as you go, until you reach the end. Brush the outside of the samosa with melted butter and place on a baking sheet. Repeat with the remaining filo strips (stacking them in pairs) and squash filling to make a total of 10 triangular samosas.

Bake in the oven for around 10–15 minutes or until golden and crisp all over, turning them over halfway through cooking. Serve the baked samosas hot or warm with the coriander chutney on the side.

Caerphilly and Chutney Rolls

These vegetarian 'sausage' rolls are based on a recipe for Glamorgan sausages – a Welsh vegetarian treat based on Caerphilly cheese. Use a different hard cheese if you prefer – Cheddar, Gruyère or Manchego are all suitable and delicious alternatives.

Makes 24 snack-size rolls (or less if you make them bigger) | Takes 25 minutes to make, 20 minutes to cook

250g Caerphilly cheese, crumbled
175g fresh wholemeal breadcrumbs
3 eggs (2 for the filling; 1 for the glaze)
1 small onion, grated
small bunch of fresh chives, snipped
plain flour, for dusting
1 pack (500g) ready-made puff pastry
about 4 tbsp favourite chutney
salt and freshly ground black pepper

Preheat the oven to 220°C/200°C fan/gas 7. Line 2 baking sheets with non-stick baking paper and set aside.

Put the cheese, breadcrumbs, 2 of the eggs and the onion into a mixing bowl and stir together until combined. Add the chives and season to taste with salt and freshly ground black pepper, making sure everything is well combined. Set aside whilst you prepare the pastry.

On a lightly floured work surface, cut the pastry into 4 equal-size pieces. Roll out each piece to form a long rectangle, each measuring around 35 x 10cm and about 3mm thick.

Divide the filling evenly between the pastry rectangles, squeezing it into a long sausage shape down the length of each strip. Using a teaspoon, dot the chutney in a line on top of the cheese filling.

Lightly beat the remaining egg. For each strip of pastry and filling, brush a little beaten egg down the sides of the pasty strip, then fold one side of the pastry up and over the filling. Brush with beaten egg, then bring the other side of pastry tightly up over the top, pressing down well to seal. Turn the whole roll over so that the sealed edges are underneath. Brush all over with the beaten egg, grinding over a little salt and black pepper, if you fancy. Repeat with the other strips

of pastry and filling to make 4 rolls.

Using a sharp knife, cut each roll into 6 equal-size pieces – or less if you want bigger rolls. Arrange the rolls, well spaced out, on the prepared baking sheets.

Bake in the oven for around 15–20 minutes or until the pastry is puffed up and deep golden brown. These vegetarian 'sausage' rolls are great served warm as part of a picnic spread, or serve them hot out of the oven with a mixed salad.

Quick Tomato, Black Olive Tapenade and Tallegio Cheese Tarts

Made during mid summer with really luscious ripe tomatoes, these speedy tarts will transport you to the Med with just one mouthful. Tallegio is a washed rind soft cheese from Italy, similar in consistency to Brie or Camembert. You can substitute any soft, melting cheese – kids in particular might favour mild oozing mozzarella to top their tarts. When I can, I also like to use a variety of mixed tomatoes – red, yellow, big, small, smooth, bumpy – as tomatoes that look interesting tend to taste interesting too.

**Makes 6 individual tarts |
Takes 15 minutes to make,
20 minutes to cook**

**plain flour, for dusting
1 pack (500g) ready-made puff
    pastry
6 heaped tsp black olive
    tapenade
500g ripe tomatoes, sliced (or
    quartered)
fresh basil leaves
200g Tallegio cheese, sliced
freshly ground black pepper**

Preheat the oven to 220°C/200°C fan/gas 7.

On a lightly floured work surface, cut the pastry into 6 equal-size pieces. Roll out each piece gently but firmly into a rectangle, about 16 x 11cm in size and about 3mm thick. Trim off the minimum to give you neat straight edges – this is not just for tidiness, as a straight edge on puff pastry helps the layers to separate and literally 'puff up' in the oven. Place on 1 or 2 baking sheets, leaving a little space around each tart. Using the tip of a sharp knife, score a shallow line about 1cm in from the edge all the way around the edge of each piece of pastry, to create a border – this will help the pastry to puff up at the edges.

Divide the tapenade between the pastry rectangles and spread evenly, keeping it within the borders. Arrange the tomato slices on top and scatter over a few basil leaves. Top each tart with slices of cheese and grind over a little black pepper.

Bake in the oven for around 20 minutes or until the pastry has puffed up and the cheese is melted and golden. Serve hot or warm. For a light snack or lunch, these tarts need no accompaniment; for a more substantial meal, you may want to serve them with an interesting salad or two.

Caramelised Pear, Walnut and Gorgonzola Tarts

Blue cheese and walnuts are a marriage made in heaven and for me they just work perfectly wherever I find them. Here they are partnered with caramelised pears on a crisp pastry base to make a lovely lunch or vegetarian starter.

Makes 6 individual tarts (ideal for a starter) | Takes 15 minutes to make (plus cooling), 25 minutes to cook

plain flour, for dusting
1 pack (500g) ready-made puff pastry
2 tbsp balsamic vinegar
1 tsp granulated sugar
3 pears, peeled, cored and cut into wedges
30g walnut pieces, roughly chopped
100g ripe Gorgonzola cheese, cubed
salt and freshly ground black pepper

On a lightly floured work surface, roll out the pastry to a thickness of about 3mm. Using a saucer as a template, cut out 6 circles, each about 15cm diameter. Using the tip of a sharp knife, score a shallow line about 1cm in from the edge all the way around the edge of each pastry circle to create a border – this will help the pastry to puff up at the edges. Arrange on 2 baking sheets, making sure there is plenty of room around each one to give it room to rise. Set aside – in the fridge if it's a hot day or on the work surface if not.

Put the balsamic vinegar and sugar into a frying pan and stir together over a medium heat until the sugar has dissolved. Reduce the heat to a minimum, add the pear wedges and toss well to coat, then cook for a couple of minutes to soften the pears slightly. Remove from the heat and set aside to cool completely.

Once the pears are cold, preheat the oven to 220°C/200°C fan/gas 7.

Arrange the pears evenly over the pastry circles, keeping them within the borders. Scatter over the walnuts and the Gorgonzola, then sprinkle over a little salt and a grind or two of black pepper.

Bake in the oven for about 20 minutes or until the pastry is crisp and cooked through and the cheese is bubbling. Serve hot or warm with a rocket salad.

Roast Squash Fatayers with Cumin-yogurt Pastry

Fatayers are delicious Middle-Eastern pastries that are filled with a variety of meat-, spinach-, cheese- or vegetable-based fillings. Here, I make them with roasted squash that is flavoured with raisins, pine nuts and coriander. Made with yogurt rather than butter, the pastry is much more healthy than shortcrust or puff and it's a doddle to make.

Makes 10 snack-size individual pastries | Takes 25 minutes to make (plus cooling and chilling), 1 hour 5 minutes to cook

For the filling
1 small butternut squash (about 700–800g), deseeded and chopped into 2cm cubes (I leave the peel on for texture)
3 tbsp olive oil
1 tsp ground cinnamon
1 tsp Spanish smoked paprika
1 tsp runny honey
75g raisins
50g pine nuts
2 cloves garlic, chopped
small bunch of fresh coriander, chopped
salt and freshly ground black pepper

For the pastry
250g plain flour, plus extra for dusting
190g full-fat natural yogurt (I use thick Greek-style yogurt)
2 tbsp extra virgin olive oil
2 tsp cumin seeds
$\frac{1}{2}$ tsp fine salt

Preheat the oven to 200°C/180°C fan/gas 6.

To make the filling, tip the squash into a roasting tin and pour over the olive oil. Add the cinnamon, paprika and honey and season generously with salt and freshly ground black pepper, tossing well to coat. Roast in the oven for 30 minutes. Stir through the raisins and pine nuts, then return to the oven for a further 10 minutes. Remove from the oven, stir through the garlic and coriander and set aside to cool completely.

Meanwhile, make the pastry. Put all the ingredients into a food processor and pulse together until the mixture resembles sticky crumbs. Tip onto a sheet of cling film and shape into a ball, pressing together well. Wrap tightly and chill in the fridge for at least 30 minutes.

Remove the pastry from the fridge and lightly dust the work surface with a little flour. Cut the pastry into 10 equal-size pieces, gently rolling each one into a ball. Roll out each ball to a circle about 3mm thick – each one should be about the size of a saucer. Brush all around the edges with a little cold water and then spoon a little filling onto one half of each circle.

For each pastry, fold over the other half of pastry to give you a half-moon shape, pressing down firmly at the edges to completely seal the filling inside.

Place on 1 or 2 baking sheets and bake in the oven for around 25 minutes or until the pastry is crisp, golden brown and cooked through. Serve hot, warm or cold. These fatayers are great dipped into some fiery harissa paste or a little hummus.

VEGETABLE

Asparagus, Gruyère and Egg Tarts

Eggs and cheese were quite possibly invented for eating with asparagus, it's just one of those flavour combinations that works perfectly. Being just a little bit generous for a starter, and perhaps not quite enough for an evening meal, these tarts make a great weekend lunch. A nice seasonal salad and a glass of wine are the perfect accompaniments.

Makes 4 individual tarts | Takes 20 minutes to make (plus chilling), 35 minutes to cook

plain flour, for dusting
1 batch of Shortcrust Pastry (see pages 6–7)
300g asparagus, woody ends trimmed off
160g Gruyère cheese, grated
4 tbsp single cream
freshly grated nutmeg, to taste
4 eggs
salt and freshly ground black pepper

Lightly dust some flour over the work surface and cut the pastry into 4 equal-size pieces, gently rolling each one into a ball. Roll out each ball to a thickness of about 3mm and use it to line an individual deep fluted loose-based tart tin (about 12cm diameter), pressing well into the base and up the sides of the tin. Take the rolling pin and give it a swift roll across the top of each tin, neatly trimming off the excess pastry, then pinch around with your thumb and forefinger to squeeze the pastry just a little higher than the top of the tins (a couple of millimetres or so) – this will allow for a little shrinkage as it cooks and creates a nice neat finish. Chill in the fridge for 20 minutes.

Meanwhile, preheat the oven to 200°C/180°C fan/gas 6.

Slide the tins onto a baking sheet and line each one with non-stick baking paper and baking beans (see page 10 for more tips on blind-baking). Bake in the oven for 15 minutes. Remove the paper and beans, then bake for a further 5 minutes to cook the pastry through completely. Remove from the oven.

Whilst the pastry is baking, prepare the filling. Blanch the asparagus in a pan of lightly salted boiling water for 3–4 minutes or until just tender but still with plenty of bite. Drain well and cool slightly. Chop off the tips to a length of about 5cm, then chop the rest of the stems into 1cm lengths. Set aside the tips and add the chopped stems to a bowl. Sprinkle in half of the cheese and pour in the cream, seasoning well with nutmeg and salt and freshly ground black pepper. Stir well, then divide evenly between the pastry cases. Arrange the asparagus tips on top around the edges of the tins in a swirl, with the tips pointing outwards. Crack an egg into the centre of each, sprinkle over the remaining cheese, then grind over a little black pepper.

Bake in the oven for around 12–15 minutes or until the eggs are set to your liking. Carefully remove the tarts from the tins to serving plates and serve hot or warm. As these tarts are rather rich, they are lovely served with an interesting leafy seasonal salad with a nice sharp dressing.

Brik a l'oeuf (Tunisian Egg Pasty)

For me these are the most perfect solitary snack, so here is a recipe just for one but feel free to scale it up to feed a crowd in more sociable moments. I have a deep-fat fryer that I use rarely, but for rustling up a little treat like this it is very handy. You can, of course, fill a pan with a deep layer of oil and fry them like that, but obviously this will be a bit more fuss just for one. Traditionally, these ubiquitous Tunisian street snacks are made from a single sheet of warka – very thin elastic pastry sheet. Warka is not that easy to source in the UK, but filo is a pretty acceptable substitute and I use 2 sheets to ensure that the precious filling has no risk of exploding out on cooking. You can also alter the filling a little. Here it's the classic egg filling, jazzed up with coriander, onion and tomatoes, but try adding some feta along with a few toasted cumin seeds, or perhaps a few slices of spicy chorizo.

Serves 1 (easily scaled up to serve a crowd) | Takes 10 minutes to make, 5 minutes to cook

vegetable oil, for deep-frying
2 sheets of filo pastry
2–3 cherry tomatoes, chopped
a few thin slivers of red or white onion
1–2 sprigs of fresh coriander, chopped
1 egg
a pinch of dried chilli flakes (optional)
salt and freshly ground black pepper

Heat some oil in an electric deep-fat fryer or in a deep frying pan to a temperature of 170°C (or until a small piece of bread browns within about 30 seconds in the hot oil).

Meanwhile, lay 1 sheet of filo pastry on the work surface and scatter the tomatoes, onion and coriander into the middle of the filo, making a slight well in the centre of the vegetables. Crack the egg into the well, season with the chilli flakes, if using, and a little salt and freshly ground black pepper. Fold the filo up over the egg, tucking in the ends and sticking them together with a little brush of cold water. You should be left with a small pasty-size parcel.

Place the parcel on the other sheet of filo and wrap it up again to give you a double layer of filo around the filling, sticking the edges together once again with a little water.

Once the oil is hot enough, lower the filo parcel into the hot oil and deep-fry for around 5 minutes or until deep golden and crisp. After this time the egg should be lightly set with an oozing yolk.

Remove the filo parcel using a slotted spoon and drain on kitchen paper. This pasty is best eaten immediately whilst piping hot and crispy. It needs no accompaniment.

Margherita Calzones (with a few extra filling ideas)

I'm not certain that Italians will classify these turnover pizzas as pies, but to my mind they are the Neapolitan equivalent to the Cornish pasty, simply made with bread dough rather than pastry. And I think they are actually quite a good thing to take on a picnic as the filling is all nicely enclosed, and surely I'm not the only one who likes a room temperature pizza rather than a scalding hot one? The beauty of these is that you can pretty much put in whatever filling takes your fancy. My kids love making pizzas, either regular flat ones or these fold-over pasty-shaped ones, I think principally because they have complete control of what goes into their meal. I simply line up a few bits and bobs in dishes and they get busy creating, their favourites being margherita with tuna for one, and margherita with ham and stoned black olives for the other. And sometimes I can persuade both of them that a little sweetcorn is a 'good thing', but not perhaps as often as I'd like.

Makes 4 calzones | Takes 25 minutes to make (plus rising), 20 minutes to cook

For the pizza dough
300ml hand-hot water
1 tsp dried yeast
a pinch of caster sugar
450g strong white bread flour
1/2 tsp salt
olive oil, for greasing

For the basic margherita filling (enough for all 4 calzones)
200g carton passata
2 x 125g balls fresh mozzarella, drained and diced into 1cm cubes
40g fresh Parmesan cheese, finely grated
small bunch of fresh basil, leaves picked and roughly torn
salt and freshly ground black pepper

To make the pizza dough, measure the hand-hot water into a jug and sprinkle over the yeast and sugar, stirring well until they have dissolved. Set aside for 10 minutes to allow the yeast a little time to wake up and activate – it should start gently bubbling. Put the flour into a mixing bowl and stir through the salt. Make a well in the centre and pour in the activated yeast liquid, using a wooden spoon to mix it together into a rough ball. Tip the dough onto the work surface and knead (using the heel of your hands to push, pull and stretch the dough) for a generous 5 minutes or so until it is smooth and stretchy. Shape the dough into a ball and place in a clean, lightly oiled bowl. Cover with cling film and set aside at room temperature for about 30 minutes to rise a little – it doesn't need to rise as much as standard bread dough.

Preheat the oven to 220°C/200°C fan/gas 7. Lightly grease 2 baking sheets and set aside.

Turn the dough onto a lightly oiled work surface and cut into 4 equal-size pieces. Roll out each piece into a circle about 5mm thick. For the filling, divide the passata evenly between the dough circles, spooning it onto one half of each circle, leaving a generous border (about 3–4cm) all around the edge. Scatter over the mozzarella and Parmesan and sprinkle over a little torn basil, then season with a little salt and freshly ground black pepper. For each calzone, fold the other half of dough over the filling, crimping and folding the edges together to firmly seal the filling inside. Arrange on the prepared baking sheets.

Bake in the oven for around 20 minutes or until crisp and deep golden brown. Remove from the oven and cool slightly before tucking in as the filling inside will be very very hot! These calzones are perfect just served on their own.

This will make you 4 delicious margherita calzones. I usually up the ante and add a few extras, not being able to resist the lure of creating something a bit more tasty. Anything goes really, just don't make the filling too wet – and try your hardest not to overfill each calzone (says someone who always does!), as you risk it bursting in the oven.

Here are a few of my favourite filling suggestions (quantities given are per calzone rather than for all 4):

Tuna, Caper and Black Olive

To the basic margherita, add a tablespoon or so of canned flaked tuna, a teaspoon or so of chopped capers, a few stoned black olives and a sprinkle of chopped fresh flat-leaf parsley.

Spicy Chorizo, Roast Red Pepper and Feta

For this one, to the basic margherita, I add a few slices of lightly-fried picante chorizo (the spicy one) and about $\frac{1}{2}$ a roasted (deseeded) red pepper, cut into strips. I'd probably leave out the mozzarella and replace it with the same weight of crumbled feta instead, but I'd still add the Parmesan for its intensive savouriness.

Caramelised Red Onion, Peas, Thyme and Goat's Cheese

I love caramelised onions (see the basic recipe for balsamic caramelised onions in the Caramelised Red Onion, Cream and Stilton Quiche recipe on page 76) – a batch of these will last for a week or so if kept covered in the fridge and they go with plenty of things, pork pie for starters. For this calzone, lose the passata and smear a generous tablespoon or two of caramelised onions in its place, then add a tablespoon of frozen peas (no need to defrost them first), followed by a sprinkling of fresh thyme leaves and a little crumbled goat's cheese in place of the mozzarella, Parmesan and basil.

Garlic Beef and Harissa

Fry a handful of minced beef in a touch of olive oil until cooked, crisp and brown. Remove from the heat and add a small crushed clove of garlic, stirring well to mix, then set aside to cool. Spoon the passata over the dough circles, then sprinkle over the minced beef mixture, dotting over a few little dollops of harissa paste (homemade or from a jar is fine). Top with the mozzarella and Parmesan and leave out the basil.

Mexican Chicken and Sweetcorn Pasties

For this spicy colourful take on a pasty, I use rough puff pastry as I really enjoy making it if I have a little time on my hands. However, they will be equally good with ready-made puff pastry to speed the process up if you prefer. The chipotle chilli sauce is optional, but I love chipotle chillies for their interesting smoky flavour – if you can't find the chilli sauce, a little Spanish smoked paprika stirred through with your favourite chilli sauce is a good substitute.

Makes 8 pasties | Takes 25 minutes to make (plus cooling), 45 minutes to cook

2 tbsp olive oil
2 large onions, finely chopped
2 large red peppers, deseeded and chopped
500g skinless boneless chicken thighs (or chicken breast if you prefer), cut into bite-size pieces
326g can sweetcorn kernels, drained
2 tbsp tomato purée
2 tsp ground cumin
2 cloves garlic, crushed
a shake of chipotle chilli sauce, to taste (optional)
generous bunch of fresh coriander, chopped
plain flour, for dusting
1 batch of Rough Puff Pastry (see pages 7–8) or use 1 pack (500g) ready-made puff pastry, if you prefer
salt and freshly ground black pepper
a little beaten egg or a mixture of milk and vegetable oil, to glaze
sea salt flakes, for sprinkling

Heat the oil in a deep frying pan and add the onions and red peppers. Fry over a medium heat for around 10–15 minutes or until starting to soften. Add the chicken, sweetcorn, tomato purée, cumin, garlic and chilli sauce, if using, stirring well to mix. Season with a little salt and freshly ground black pepper and continue to fry for a further 10 minutes or so until the chicken is cooked through – cut one of the largest pieces open to check it's cooked.

Remove from the heat and set aside to cool completely – spreading the mixture out on a shallow dish or tray will speed this up considerably. Once cold, stir through the coriander, and taste to check the seasoning, adding a little more salt and black pepper, if necessary.

Once the filling is cold, preheat the oven to 220°C/200°C fan/gas 7.

Dust the work surface with a little flour. Cut the pastry into 8 equal-size pieces, pressing each one into a rough ball as you do so. Roll out each ball into a circle about the size of a side plate and about 3mm thick. Spoon some of the filling into the centre of each pastry circle, dividing evenly, then brush a little cold water around the edges. Bring up the sides of each pastry circle so they meet at the top, crimping and folding the edges together to completely seal the filling inside. Brush with a little beaten egg or a mixture of milk and oil and sprinkle over a few sea salt flakes. Arrange the pasties on 2 baking sheets, leaving enough space between each one to allow them to cook and rise evenly.

Bake in the oven for around 20 minutes or until the pastry is crisp and golden. These pasties are great served hot or warm, either on their own as a good picnic snack, or perhaps with some guacamole to spoon over as you eat.

Turkey, Brie and Cranberry Turnovers

These are lovely lunch-size snacks that make the most of the post-Christmas leftovers. This recipe can very easily be scaled up or down or adapted to suit what you might have lurking in the fridge. Try it with a different cheese – Stilton is a good alternative – or with a little shredded cooked ham. Spicy chutney in lieu of cranberry sauce is another great tweak.

Makes 8 turnovers | Takes 20 minutes to make, 30 minutes to cook

plain flour, for dusting
1 pack (500g) ready-made puff
    pastry
8 tsp cranberry sauce
250–300g cooked cold turkey
    (or chicken), cubed
250–300g Brie, cubed
few fresh sage leaves, finely
    shredded
1 egg, lightly beaten
salt and freshly ground black
    pepper

Preheat the oven to 220°C/200°C fan/gas 7.

On a lightly floured work surface, cut the pastry into 8 equal-size pieces. Roll each piece gently but firmly into a square, about 3mm thick. Spoon the cranberry sauce onto half of each square, leaving a generous 1cm border all around the edge of each one – you will be folding them over into triangles, so arrange your filling with that shape in mind.

Scatter the turkey and Brie onto the cranberry sauce, sprinkle over the sage and grind over a little salt and freshly ground black pepper. Brush a little beaten egg all around the border of each square and bring up the pastry to enclose the filling and make a triangular parcel, pressing down firmly at the edges to seal the filling inside. Take a sharp knife and trim the edges of each triangle to neaten it up, then brush all over the tops with a little more beaten egg. Place the finished turnovers on a couple of baking sheets, making sure they have plenty of room between them to puff up during cooking.

Bake in the oven for 25–30 minutes or until the pastry is crisp, puffed up and golden. Serve hot with plenty of salad and pickles.

Moroccan-spiced Chicken and Almond Briouats ('Cigars')

These large spring roll-shaped pastries are stuffed with a rich spiced chicken filling, the inspiration for which is the famous Moroccan 'pastilla'. Traditionally made from pigeon, eggs and almonds, and very sweet with honey and cinnamon – almost like a dessert – I find pastilla just a bit too rich. My filling is most definitely savoury and these make a great lunch or snack, or a splendid start to a North African feast. Use any leftover sheets of filo to make yourself a gorgeous Brik a l'oeuf (see page 114) for lunch.

Makes 8 briouats (serves 4 for lunch or more as a starter) | Takes 25 minutes to make (plus cooling), 1 hour 20 minutes to cook

a pinch of saffron threads
2 tbsp boiling water
2 tbsp olive oil
25g unsalted butter
3 skin-on, bone-in chicken thighs
2 red onions, chopped
2 green peppers, deseeded and chopped
2 cloves garlic, crushed
1 tbsp runny honey
1 tsp ground ginger
1 tsp ground cinnamon
1 tsp chilli powder, or to taste
$\frac{1}{2}$ tsp ground turmeric
1 lemon, cut lengthways into quarters
100g (drained weight) stoned green olives, drained and roughly chopped
100g blanched almonds, roughly chopped
small bunch of fresh flat-leaf parsley, chopped
small bunch of fresh coriander, chopped
8 sheets of filo pastry from a 250g pack
50g butter, melted

salt and freshly ground black pepper

Sprinkle the saffron into a small heatproof glass or cup and pour over the boiling water. Set aside to soak, whilst you prepare the filling.

Put the oil and unsalted butter into a deep, heavy-based frying pan and set over a medium-high heat. Once the butter starts foaming, add the chicken thighs, skin-side down, and fry first on one side, then on the other until golden and a little crispy – this will take about 8–10 minutes in total. The butter will start to caramelise to a nutty brown, which adds a lovely flavour, although reduce the heat if it looks like it might burn.

Reduce the heat to as low as possible and add the onions, green peppers and garlic, mixing well. Stir through the honey, along with all the ground spices, then squeeze over the lemon quarters, tucking in the empty shells as you go. Finally, stir through the olives and almonds and the saffron threads and their soaking water. Season with a little salt and freshly ground black pepper. Cover with a lid or snug-fitting piece of foil and cook gently for around 45 minutes or until the chicken is fully cooked,

stirring once or twice.

Remove from the heat, then remove the chicken pieces to a plate and leave to cool a little before shredding the meat and returning it to the pan. Discard the skin and bones. Remove and discard the lemon shells, and then stir through the parsley and coriander. Taste to check the seasoning, adding a little more salt and black pepper, if necessary. Set aside to cool completely – spreading the mixture out on a shallow tray will speed this up considerably.

Once the filling is cold, preheat the oven to 200°C/180°C fan/gas 6.

Roughly divide the filling into 8 equal-size portions, either on the tray you cooled it on or on a large plate (each portion will be around 2 tablespoons). For each briouat, unroll one of the sheets of filo onto a clean dry work surface and lay it lengthways with the longest edge nearest to you (cover the rest of the pastry with a clean damp tea towel to keep it supple). Assuming you are right-handed and working left to right, spoon the filling a few centimetres from the left hand edge, leaving a generous 5cm border at the top and the bottom – you are aiming for a fat sausage shape. Brush a little melted butter along the top and bottom borders, then first fold one border, then the other, up over the filling, covering it up completely. Then, roll the briouat up into a spring roll shape, just like rolling up a carpet. Once you get to the end, brush on a little more melted butter to seal it all together, then brush a little more all over before placing the briouat on a baking sheet. Repeat with the remaining filo pastry sheets and filling to make 8 briouats in total.

Bake in the oven for around 20 minutes or until the pastry is crisp and golden. Serve hot or warm. A little smear of harissa paste as you eat is delicious with these pastries.

Creamed Celeriac, Serrano Ham and Parmesan Tartlets

These elegant little tartlets make a great dinner party starter. To keep the pastry crisp, fill them just before you grill them, and for best results, make sure the celeriac purée is piping hot throughout before adding it to the cases.

Makes 6 individual tartlets (ideal for a starter) | Takes 25 minutes to make (plus chilling), 25 minutes to cook

plain flour, for dusting
1 batch of Parmesan Shortcrust Pastry (see pages 6–7)
juice of $1/2$ lemon
300g celeriac (about $1/2$ a medium one)
50–75ml double cream
1 tbsp chopped fresh flat-leaf parsley
6 thin slices Serrano ham
25g fresh Parmesan cheese, finely grated
salt and freshly ground black pepper

Lightly dust some flour over the work surface and cut the pastry into 6 equal-size pieces, gently rolling each one into a ball. Roll out each ball to a thickness of about 3mm and use it to line an individual shallow loose-based tartlet tin (about 10cm diameter), pressing well into the base and up the sides of the tin, but taking care not to stretch the pastry too much or it will shrink on cooking. Take the rolling pin and give it a swift roll across the top of each tin, neatly trimming off the excess pastry, then pinch around with your thumb and forefinger to squeeze the pastry just a little higher than the top of the tins (a couple of millimetres or so) – this will allow for a little shrinkage as it cooks and creates a nice neat finish. Chill in the fridge for 20 minutes.

Meanwhile, preheat the oven to 200°C/180°C fan/gas 6.

Slide the tins onto a baking sheet and line each one with non-stick baking paper and baking beans (see page 10 for more tips on blind-baking). Bake in the oven for 15 minutes. Remove the paper and beans, then bake for a further 5 minutes to cook the pastry through completely. Remove from the oven and set aside.

Meanwhile, fill a bowl with cold water and add the lemon juice. Peel the celeriac and then cut the flesh into 2–3cm cubes, dropping it into the lemony water as you go – this will stop it oxidising and turning brown. Bring a pan of lightly salted water to the boil, then drain the celeriac and immediately add it to the pan. Bring back to the boil, then boil until the celeriac is tender, around 15 minutes, perhaps a touch more or less, depending on the size you cut the celeriac.

Drain well and return to the pan. Mash thoroughly, adding the cream and salt and freshly ground black pepper to taste. For a really smooth texture, push the mixture through a fine sieve and then reheat until piping hot throughout. At this point you can also cool and chill the purée in the fridge, ready for reheating when you are ready to eat, if you like.

Preheat the grill to high.

Carefully remove the tartlet cases from the tins. Divide the hot celeriac purée between the tartlet cases, sprinkle over a little parsley and top each one with a crumpled slice of Serrano ham. Scatter the Parmesan over the top, then flash under the hot grill for just a minute or so until the cheese just begins to crisp. Transfer the tartlets to serving plates and serve immediately. As a starter, these really need no accompaniment, but serve with a seasonal salad for a more substantial meal.

Beef Burger Patties

When I sat down to start writing this book, I spent some time pondering all the memorable pies of my past, and variations of these 'historical' pies are dotted throughout this book. But this – the beef burger patty – has perhaps my most vivid pie memories, it being the one most connected to my teenage years. School used to serve these up at morning break, and again at lunch, and they disappeared like hot cakes. They were guaranteed to be scorching, so you had trouble not burning your tongue as you scoffed greedily, always keeping one eye on what the boys were doing on the other side of the playground. Each patty basically comprises a burger topped with pickle, which is then sandwiched between layers of puff pastry. These are (hopefully) way too unhealthy for school dinners these days, but as a once in a while savoury treat they are rather perfect.

Makes 4 patties | Takes 20 minutes to make (plus cooling), 40 minutes to cook

450g minced beef
1 small onion, grated
1 heaped tsp Marmite
pinch of dried mixed herbs
plain flour, for dusting
1 pack (500g) ready-made puff pastry
4 heaped tsp pickle (use your favourite one – it was always Branston Pickle at school!)
salt and freshly ground black pepper
1 tbsp milk mixed with 1 tbsp vegetable oil, to glaze

In a mixing bowl, squish together the minced beef, onion, Marmite and dried herbs. Season well with salt and freshly ground black pepper, then divide the mixture into 4 equal-size balls. Flatten each one into a disc about 1cm thick – it will be around 10–12cm diameter.

Heat a griddle pan to smoking hot (or preheat a barbecue). Add the patties to the hot pan and cook over a high heat for around 3 minutes on each side or until the outsides are nicely caramelised and the burgers are cooked through. Remove from the heat and set the burgers aside on a plate to cool completely.

Once the burgers are cold, preheat the oven to 220°C/200°C fan/gas 7.

On a lightly floured work surface, cut the pastry into 8 equal-size pieces. Roll out each piece to a rough circle that is about 3mm thick and about 2cm or so bigger than the cooked burger (which will have shrunk a little on cooking). Lay a burger in the centre of each pastry disc and spoon a dollop of pickle into the middle. Brush a little water around the borders of pastry and then lay a second disc of pastry over each burger, pressing down firmly all around the edges to seal the burger inside. Use a small sharp knife to trim all around the edges, pierce a little hole in the top of each patty and then brush all over with the milk and oil mixture to glaze. Place on a baking sheet, leaving plenty of room between each one.

Bake in the oven for around 30 minutes or until puffed up, golden and crisp. These patties are best served piping hot and eaten with your hands, just as they are. They need no accompaniment.

Jamaican Patties

These tropical patties are a glorious deep yellow colour – courtesy of the turmeric – and they are filled with a lightly-spiced curry of mince and vegetables. For some reason, the turmeric seems to make the pastry a little fragile and delicate, which is a bit surprising as it only contains a teaspoonful. Just work with the pastry quickly but gently, patching up and pressing together any cracks as they appear, and using a dab of cold water, if necessary.

Makes 6 patties | Takes 25 minutes to make (plus chilling and cooling), 1 hour 20 minutes to cook

For the pastry
450g plain flour, plus extra for dusting
1 tsp ground turmeric
¹/₂ tsp fine salt
225g butter, cut into 1cm dice
about 8 tbsp ice-cold water

For the filling
1 tbsp olive oil
400g minced beef
2 carrots, finely chopped
1 large onion, finely chopped
1 red pepper, deseeded and finely chopped
2 cloves garlic, crushed
1 tsp curry paste (any variety of your choice)
a pinch of dried thyme
400g can chopped tomatoes
salt and freshly ground black pepper

To make the pastry, put the flour, turmeric and salt into a food processor and whizz together, or mix together by hand in a large mixing bowl. If you are using a food processor, add the butter and pulse until the mixture resembles coarse breadcrumbs. If you are making it by hand, rub the butter into the flour between your thumbs and fingers until the mixture resembles coarse breadcrumbs. Add just enough ice-cold water to bring the mixture together into loose clumps, then tip onto a sheet of cling film and press gently into a fat sausage shape. Wrap, then chill in the fridge whilst you make the filling.

For the filling, pour the oil into a deep frying pan and set over a high heat. Add the minced beef and fry for about 10 minutes or until lightly browned, stirring occasionally to break it up. Reduce the temperature a little, then add the carrots, onion and red pepper, along with the garlic, curry paste and thyme and fry for a further 10 minutes, stirring every now and then.

Pour in the tomatoes and 200ml cold water and season with salt and freshly ground black pepper. Bring to a simmer, then simmer steadily, uncovered, for around 20–30 minutes or until the sauce is reduced and really quite thick, stirring occasionally. Remove from the heat, taste to check the seasoning, adding a little more salt and black pepper, if necessary, then set aside to cool completely – spreading the mixture out on a shallow tray will speed this up considerably.

Once the filling is cold, preheat the oven to 200°C/180°C fan/gas 6.

On a lightly floured work surface, cut the pastry into 6 equal-size pieces, gently rolling each one into a ball. Roll out each ball into a circle about the size of a side plate and about 3mm thick. Brush all around the edges with a little cold water and then spoon some filling onto one half of each circle, leaving a generous 1cm border all around the edge. For each patty, bring the pastry up and over the filling, pressing down firmly at the edges to completely seal the filling inside. Trim each patty with a sharp knife to give you a neat 'D' shape, then take a fork and press down all around the sealed edge to give you a traditional finish. Place the patties on a baking sheet.

Bake in the oven for around 25–30 minutes or until the pastry feels crisp and cooked to the touch – this pastry won't really brown like traditional shortcrust pastry. Serve hot or warm. These patties are best eaten with your hands! They are perfect as they are and need no accompaniment.

Gammon and Leek Slices

The inspiration for these was those cheese and ham slices you can buy in the bakers – you know the ones, where there's very little evidence of ham and simply not enough cheese to make it cheesy. Often tempting, always disappointing. These then are the real deal, with plenty of tasty filling surrounded by crisp herby pastry. For a bit more punch, you can add a teaspoon or so of Dijon mustard to the filling as it thickens, if you like.

**Makes 6 individual slices |
Takes 25 minutes to make
(plus cooling),1 hour to cook**

1 tbsp olive oil
25g unsalted butter
3 leeks, washed and sliced
**2 tbsp plain flour, plus extra
    for dusting**
350ml milk
**75g mature Cheddar cheese,
    grated**
250g cooked gammon, diced
**1¹/₂ batches of Herby Rough
    Puff Pastry (see pages 7–8)**
**salt and freshly ground black
    pepper**
a little beaten egg, to glaze
**sea salt flakes, for sprinkling
    (optional)**

Put the oil and butter into a heavy-based saucepan and set over a low heat. Once the butter has melted, add the leeks, stirring well to coat. Scrunch up a sheet of greaseproof paper and briefly rinse it under running water. Shake off the excess water, then lay the dampened paper over the leeks, tucking it under snugly at the edges. This creates a steamy lid that will help the leeks soften without colouring. Sweat the leeks gently for around 15 minutes or until they are soft and tender, lifting the paper to stir occasionally.

Discard the paper and then sprinkle in the flour, stirring well to mix it into the buttery juices. Gradually pour in the milk, stirring all the time to prevent lumps forming as the sauce begins to thicken. Bring gently to the boil, then simmer steadily for about 5 minutes to cook the flour. Remove from the heat, stir through the cheese and season to taste with salt and freshly ground black pepper. Set aside to cool completely. Once cold, stir through the cooked gammon.

Once the filling is cold, preheat the oven to 220°C/200°C fan/gas 7.

On a lightly floured work surface, cut the pastry into 2 pieces, making one piece slightly larger than the other. Roll out the smaller piece into a large rectangle about 3mm thick. Cut the rectangle in half lengthways, and then cut each piece widthways into 3, giving you 6 rectangles, each about 12 x 16cm. Don't worry too much if yours are not these dimensions – squares will be OK too, just try to make them similar sizes. Arrange on 2 heavy baking sheets.

Spoon some filling into the middle of each pastry rectangle, dividing it evenly, leaving a generous 1cm border all around the edge of each one. Brush a little cold water on the pastry borders.

Take the other piece of pastry and once again roll it out into a large rectangle that is about 3mm thick. Cut it into 6 similar-shaped rectangles as before, making each one just a little larger than the bases to ensure they enclose the filling. Lay the pastry tops over the filling, pressing down firmly to seal the edges. Use a small sharp knife to trim and neaten the edges – a clean straight line will allow the pastry to puff up a little better in the oven. Cut a couple of slits in the top of each one. Brush all over with beaten egg, then sprinkle with a few sea salt flakes, if you like.

Bake in the oven for 30–35 minutes or until golden brown and cooked through. Serve hot or warm. These slices really need nothing to serve alongside them and they are best, I think, when eaten piping hot from the oven – not quite so hot that they burn you, but nearly that hot!

Cornish Pasties

As a Cornish-born lass, I must admit to a bit of a weakness for a proper pasty, one packed to bursting with steak, potato and swede and laced with plenty (and I do mean plenty) of black pepper. The crust is traditionally made with strong white bread flour, the high gluten content of which creates a strong elastic dough that's man enough to support the robust filling inside. It may seem that you are using rather a lot of flour, but you need a generous quantity to form the all-important roll-over crust. Just don't crimp your crust on top, it has to be rolled and twisted along the sealed edge (like a rope) on one side, otherwise it's a Devon pasty not a Cornish one. Apparently.

Makes 6 pasties | Takes 30 minutes to make (plus chilling), 50 minutes to cook

For the pastry
600g strong white bread flour, plus extra for dusting
150g butter, cut into 1cm dice
150g lard or vegetable shortening, cut into 1cm dice
1 tsp fine salt
about 16–18 tbsp ice-cold water

For the filling
400g skirt beef, cut into 1cm cubes
400g waxy potatoes, peeled and cut into 1cm cubes
300g swede, peeled and cut into 1cm cubes
1 onion, chopped
30g butter
salt and freshly ground black pepper

1 egg, lightly beaten, to glaze
sea salt flakes, for sprinkling (optional)

To make the pastry, put the flour, butter, lard and salt into a large mixing bowl and stir together. Gradually add just enough ice-cold water to bring it all together into a firm dough that is not too sticky. There should be no loose pieces of fat or flour left in the bowl. Turn the pastry onto a lightly floured work surface and roll out to form a rectangle about 1cm thick. With a short edge nearest to you, fold the top third down towards you into the middle, and then fold the bottom third up over it – just like folding a letter. Give the pastry a quarter turn (turn it 90 degrees) so that the folded edges are at the sides, then roll it out to a rectangle again (same size as before) and repeat the folding. Repeat this turning, rolling and folding process 4 or 5 times, keeping the work surface and rolling pin lightly floured. Wrap the pastry in cling film and chill in the fridge for at least 1 hour before using.

For the filling, in a bowl, mix together the beef, potatoes, swede and onion and season really generously with salt and freshly ground black pepper. Cover and set aside for the flavours to mingle whilst the pastry is chilling – in the fridge on a hot day, or on a cool work surface is fine if it's a cooler day.

Preheat the oven to 200°C/180°C fan/gas 6.

On a lightly floured work surface, cut the pastry into 6 equal-size pieces, gently rolling each piece into a rough ball as you go. Roll out each ball into a circle about 5mm thick – it will be bigger than a side plate, but not quite as big as a dinner plate. Divide the filling evenly between the pastry circles, spooning it onto one half of each circle, leaving a generous 3cm border all around the edge. Dot the butter on top of the filling. Brush all around the edges with a little cold water. For each pasty, fold the other half of pastry over the filling, enclosing it completely. Press the two edges of pastry together firmly, then twist all along the edge like a rope to seal the edge. Brush all over with a little beaten egg to glaze, then sprinkle over a few sea salt flakes, if you fancy.

Arrange the pasties on 2 baking sheets and put them into the hot oven. Immediately reduce the oven temperature to 180°C/160°C fan/gas 4 and bake for around 50 minutes or until cooked and deep golden brown. These pasties are best served hot from the oven, or leave them to cool to room temperature, if you prefer. They need no accompaniment and are perfect just served on their own.

Apple and Leftover Pork Pasties

These pasties were originally made to use up some leftover roast pork and gravy one miserable Monday lunchtime, and they certainly hit the spot. Nicer and infinitely more satisfying than yet another sandwich. I have given the quantities for two pasties as that's what I made but it's a recipe that is very easily scaled up, and I'd go as far as to say make sure you cook plenty of pork and extra gravy just so you can make them. I use a little fresh rosemary as I have a bush near the back door so it's completely free. If you don't have rosemary in your garden, don't buy a whole pack from the supermarket just for this recipe as you only need a little try using a little pinch of dried mixed herbs instead.

Makes 2 generous-size pasties (easily scaled up to feed more) | Takes 20 minutes to make, 30 minutes to cook

plain flour, for dusting
1 batch of Shortcrust Pastry (see pages 6–7)
120g chopped (peeled and cored) Bramley apple (about ½ an apple) (or use leftover cold apple sauce, if you have some, but don't add the sugar)
1 tsp caster sugar
160g leftover cold cooked pork, roughly chopped
1 tsp finely chopped fresh rosemary leaves
4 tbsp leftover cold gravy
salt and freshly ground black pepper
1 tbsp milk mixed with 1 tbsp vegetable oil, to glaze
sea salt flakes, for sprinkling

Preheat the oven to 200°C/180°C fan/gas 6.

On a lightly floured work surface, cut the pastry in half and roll each piece into a ball. Roll out each ball into a rough circle about the size of a side plate and about 3mm thick – starting with a ball of pastry will help it turn out more circular as you roll.

In a bowl toss the apple pieces in the caster sugar, add the pork and rosemary, then season with salt and freshly ground black pepper and stir well. Divide this mixture evenly between the 2 pastry circles, spooning it into the middle of each one. Spoon half of the gravy onto the filling of one pasty and quickly bring up the sides so they meet at the top, crimping and folding the edges to seal the pasty all around. Repeat to make the other pasty, again making sure the filling is well and truly sealed in its pastry case. Brush the combined milk and oil glaze all over each pasty. Sprinkle with a few flakes of sea salt and then slide carefully onto a baking sheet.

Bake in the oven for around 30 minutes or until the pastry is crisp and golden. Serve hot or warm. These pasties don't really need any other accompaniment, but for a more substantial meal, serve with a side salad.

PORK

Sausage Rolls with Onion Chutney and Caraway Seeds

I love making sausage rolls at Christmas. For me they feel just as festive as mince pies and everyone seems to love them, but they are equally good at any sort of party. I always use skinned sausages rather than plain sausagemeat, as I find they have more flavour. This recipe was a bit of an experiment because I added a little layer of onion chutney underneath the sausages to make for an easy eating all-in-one bite. It works really well, with the onions oozing and caramelising deliciously, but avoid the temptation to be too overgenerous or it will have a tendency to bubble out just a little too much. Lining your baking sheets with non-stick baking paper will make washing up easier too!

Makes about 24 snack-size sausage rolls (recipe easily doubles up for a crowd) | Takes 25 minutes to make, 20 minutes to cook

plain flour, for dusting
1 pack (500g) ready-made puff pastry
about half a (340g) jar of onion chutney
12 chipolata sausages
1 egg, lightly beaten
2 tsp caraway seeds
sea salt flakes, for sprinkling

Preheat the oven to 220°C/200°C fan/gas 7. Line 2 baking sheets with non-stick baking paper and set aside.

On a lightly floured work surface, roll out the pastry to form a rectangle about 30 x 40cm in size and about 3mm thick. Cut into quarters lengthways to give you four equal-size long thin rectangles or strips (each about 30 x 10cm in size). Spread a layer of onion chutney down the middle of each strip. Using a small sharp knife, carefully score a line through the skin of each sausage. Peel away the skins, leaving the sausages as intact as possible.

Lay 3 of the skinned sausages end-to-end over the chutney on one strip of pastry, packing them as close together as possible. Fold one side of the pastry up and over the sausages. Brush well with beaten egg, then bring the other side of pastry tightly up over the top, pressing down well to seal. Turn the whole roll over so that the sealed edges are underneath. Repeat with the other strips of pastry and the rest of the sausages.

Brush all over with more egg to glaze, then sprinkle over the caraway seeds and a few sea salt flakes. Cut each roll widthways into about 6 equal-size pieces. Finally, using a pair of kitchen scissors, snip through the top of each sausage roll 2 or 3 times to make pretty holes to let the steam out. Arrange the sausage rolls, well spaced out, on the prepared baking sheets.

Bake in the oven for about 20 minutes or until cooked and deep golden brown. These are best served whilst still warm and they are great just as they are – no accompaniment needed.

SWEET PIES

Is there anything better than being presented with a homemade pie or tart for pudding? I simply cannot think of a pudding I'd rather eat than a simple, home-baked apple pie – hot sweet fruit, perhaps with a hint of spice, wrapped in crisply baked buttery pastry and then eaten with a generous drizzle of cold, cold cream or piping hot custard (or even cold custard if you prefer, as I do). My idea of heaven on a plate. But why stop at apple pie, when there is a whole world of delicious sweet pies out there… from delicious open tarts and strudels, to fruity tartlets and zesty pies, or individual sugary confections full of caramelised nuts or creamy toffee. Here, you will find a wealth of delicious sweet treats perfect for sharing.

Classic Bakewell Tart

This classic English tart, hailing from Bakewell in Derbyshire, can be described as a sort of soft almond cake inside a crisp pastry tart case, the pastry's role simply being to support the delicate buttery filling it encases. Feel free to vary the jam: here I have plumped for traditional raspberry, but something sharp like blackcurrant will be equally delicious.

Serves 8 | Takes 20 minutes to make (plus cooling), 35 minutes to cook

4–5 heaped tbsp raspberry jam
1 deep 25cm blind-baked Shortcrust Pastry Tart Case (see pages 6–7)
200g ground almonds
200g butter, cut into 1cm cubes
200g caster sugar
3 eggs
1 tsp almond extract (or vanilla extract, if you prefer)
50g flaked almonds
icing sugar, for dusting

Preheat the oven to 200°C/180°C fan/gas 6.

Spread the jam evenly over the base of the pastry tart case. Put the ground almonds, butter, caster sugar, eggs and almond extract into a food processor and whizz everything together to form a smooth paste. You can also do this with a hand-held electric mixer or a freestanding food mixer, or by hand with a strong arm and a wooden spoon if the butter is softened a little first. Spoon the creamed mixture evenly over the jam and level with the flat of a table knife or palette knife, then sprinkle over the flaked almonds.

Bake in the oven for around 30–35 minutes or until the filling has set and is golden brown on top. If the top is browning too quickly, cover loosely with foil towards the end of cooking.

Remove from the oven and leave to cool to room temperature. Carefully remove the tart from the tin and transfer it to a serving plate. Dust over a little icing sugar before serving. Serve on its own or with a drizzle of cream.

Apricot and Almond Tart

Though perhaps not so fashionable these days, I think canned apricots, providing they are canned in juice, are a really good thing to eat. In this easy French-style tart, they are baked with an almondy custard to make a lovely dessert or afternoon tea treat.

Serves 6–8 | Takes 15 minutes to make (plus cooling), 30 minutes to cook

2 eggs
2 egg yolks
100g caster sugar
250ml milk
50g ground almonds
1/2 tsp almond extract
420g can apricot halves in juice, drained
1 shallow 25cm blind-baked Shortcrust Pastry Tart Case (see pages 6–7)
40g flaked almonds

Preheat the oven to 180°C/160°C fan/gas 4.

In a mixing bowl, whisk the eggs, egg yolks and sugar together until slightly thickened. Add the milk, ground almonds and almond extract and whisk together until completely combined.

Arrange the apricot halves, cut-sides down, over the base of the pastry tart case. Carefully pour in the egg and almond mixture, allowing it to flow around the apricots. Sprinkle over the flaked almonds.

Bake in the oven for around 30 minutes or until just set. Remove from the oven and leave to cool a little. Carefully remove the tart from the tin to a serving plate. Serve just warm or cold, perhaps with a drizzle of cream, if you fancy.

Baklava

Ridiculously sweet but very moreish, this nutty filo pie is best served in small pieces, making it the perfect thing to serve with coffee at the end of a meal. Luckily, baklava keeps really well – for at least a week in an airtight container – so you need not feel obliged to eat lots in one sitting! I've kept the flavourings of rosewater and orange blossom water quite subtle as I like the taste of the nuts to shine through, but you can add more if you fancy.

Makes 1 batch, which cuts into around 30 bite-size pieces | Takes 25 minutes to make (plus cooling), 40 minutes to cook

melted butter, for greasing

For the syrup
350g granulated sugar
75g runny honey
1 tbsp orange blossom water (orange flower water)
1 tbsp rosewater

For the nuts and pastry
200g pistachios (shelled weight)
200g walnut pieces
1 pack (250g) filo pastry (about 10 sheets)
75g butter, melted

Preheat the oven to 200°C/180°C fan/gas 6. Grease a shallow 20 x 30cm cake tin with a little melted butter and set aside.

First, make the syrup. Put the sugar and 150ml cold water into a heavy-based saucepan. Set the pan over a medium heat and bring up to the boil, stirring just until the sugar has dissolved, then leave to steadily simmer away for 5 minutes. Remove from the heat and pour into a heatproof jug, then stir through the honey, orange blossom water and rosewater. Set aside, loosely covered.

For the nuts, put the pistachios and walnuts into a food processor and whizz until finely ground. Set aside.

For the pastry, unroll the filo pastry onto the work surface (keep it covered with a clean damp tea towel to keep it supple). Take a sheet of filo and place it in the prepared tin, pressing it firmly into the corners, then brush it all over with a little melted butter. Using about half of the pack of filo, continue layering the sheets, one on top of the other, brushing each one with melted butter – stagger the layers of filo pastry if necessary (depending on the size of your tin and filo sheets) to give you an even base of pastry completely covering the base and up the sides of the tin and overhanging the top edges of the tin by a few millimetres or so.

Tip the ground nuts into the filo-lined tin, spreading them evenly and pressing down lightly with the back of a spoon. Use the rest of the filo sheets to cover the nuts, again layering each sheet on top of each other (staggering them again, if necessary) and brushing each one with melted butter, as before. Brush the top sheet of filo with a final slick of butter, then use a sharp knife to cut the pie into small squares or diamond shapes. You will need to cut all the way through the pastry and nuts, right through to the bottom – this is far easier than it might sound, but you may need to support the top layers of pastry with one hand as you cut with the other. Finally, trim away any excess pastry hanging over the sides – I find this job easiest with a pair of kitchen scissors.

Bake in the oven for around 30 minutes, by which time the pastry should be deep golden brown and crisp. Remove from the oven, then slowly and evenly pour over the syrup whilst the pastry is still hot. Set aside to cool completely before serving. Serve cold, cut into small bite-size pieces. Store any leftovers in an airtight container at room temperature for up to a week.

Gypsy Tart

To me this is an extremely nostalgic tart – I remember eating Gypsy Tart as a schoolgirl many moons ago. It's a regional speciality from Kent, and is virtually unknown elsewhere in the UK, so once I moved to a different part of the country aged 10, I simply never ate it again. That is until I made my own. It's so simple to make (just a handful of ingredients is all you need), I wonder why it has taken me 30 years to get around to it. It is probably best described as a sort of butterscotch mousse in a crisp pastry case, very sweet but very delicious. It is important to whisk the filling for a good few minutes to aerate it, otherwise it won't have the light fluffy texture it should.

Serves 6–8 | Takes 15 minutes to make (plus cooling), 15 minutes to cook

2 small cans (170g each) evaporated milk
275g light muscovado sugar
1 shallow 25cm blind-baked Shortcrust Pastry Tart Case (see pages 6–7)

Preheat the oven to 200°C/180°C fan/gas 6.

Either in a freestanding food mixer or in a large bowl using a hand-held electric whisk, whisk together the evaporated milk and sugar until the mixture is pale, fluffy and studded with air bubbles. This will take around 10 minutes and is an important step for a light fluffy texture. Pour the filling into the pastry tart case, then slide the tin onto a baking sheet.

Bake in the oven for about 15 minutes or until the surface is a caramel brown colour and almost dry but still slightly tacky on the surface. Remove from the oven and leave to cool completely in the tin.

Carefully remove the tart from the tin to a serving plate. Serve at room temperature. This tart is best served just as it is. Cream, I think, will be overkill for this super sweet pie, though you may disagree.

Egg Custard Tarts

For these simple egg custard tarts, I like to add freshly grated nutmeg to flavour the pastry as I make it. Simply grate half a nutmeg or so into the flour and butter crumbs before you add the water. With these small tarts, I find that it's important to let the pastry relax in the fridge after rolling and pressing it into the tin. Because they are little, you really notice if the pastry shrinks on baking, and if it shrinks too much it's hard to get all the filling in.

Makes 12 individual tarts | Takes 25 minutes to make (plus chilling), 30 minutes to cook

plain flour, for dusting
1 batch of Sweet Shortcrust Pastry (see pages 6–7, and flavoured with grated nutmeg if you like – see recipe intro above)
2 eggs
2 egg yolks (save the whites for a different recipe)
50g caster sugar
250ml single cream
freshly grated nutmeg, for sprinkling

On a lightly floured work surface, roll out the pastry to a thickness of about 3mm. Open out a paper muffin case, pressing it flat, and use it as a template to cut out 12 circles. If necessary, reshape and re-roll the scraps of pastry to get the 12 circles you need. Press each circle gently but firmly into the holes in a 12-hole muffin tin and prick all over with a fork (this helps prevent the pastry from puffing up in the oven). Leave to rest in the fridge for 30 minutes to relax the pastry and reduce shrinkage during baking.

Once the pastry cases are rested, preheat the oven to 200°C/180°C fan/gas 6.

Bake the pastry cases in the oven for around 10–15 minutes or until just cooked through. Check halfway through baking and if the cases are puffing up a lot, remove from the oven and press the pastry back down before continuing to bake. (You can blind-bake them with non-stick baking paper and beans, just as you would do with a large case – see page 10 for more tips on this – but it's such a fiddle to do this with small tarts like these that I prefer to do it like this.) Once baked, remove from the oven.

To make the filling, in a mixing bowl, whisk together the eggs, egg yolks and sugar until slightly thickened, then whisk in the cream. Transfer the mixture to a jug, then pour the mixture into the baked pastry cases, dividing it evenly. Sprinkle over plenty of freshly grated nutmeg. Return to the oven and bake for a further 15 minutes or so until the custard is just set but with a slight wobble in the middle.

Remove from the oven and leave to cool just a little before using a table knife to help you release the tarts from the tins. Serve these tarts just as they are, preferably warm from the oven.

Old-fashioned Apple Pie

I'm sure many people feel they don't need a recipe for a simple apple pie. It's possibly the first thing many of us learned to cook by ourselves, taught at school, or at home by our mothers or grandmothers, or indeed our fathers. So, apologies in advance if I'm 'teaching you to suck eggs', but it's such a complete classic, I felt I couldn't write a book on pies without including a recipe for apple pie. Everyone has a slightly different approach, this just happens to be mine and it is one of my very favourite puddings in the world. For me, little can beat the contrast between hot sweet-but-tart apple pie and cold, cold double cream.

Serves 6 | Takes 20 minutes to make (plus cooling), 1 hour 10 minutes to cook

100g granulated sugar
1kg Bramley apples
1 tsp cornflour
plain flour, for dusting
double batch of Shortcrust Pastry (see pages 6–7)
a little beaten egg or a mixture of milk and vegetable oil, to glaze
a little granulated or caster sugar, for sprinkling

Measure 200ml cold water into a large saucepan and add the granulated sugar. Bring to a simmer and then reduce the heat to as low as possible. Peel and core the apples, then chop into 2–3cm dice, dropping them into the hot sweetened water as you go to prevent them from discolouring. Simmer gently, uncovered, for around 10 minutes or until the apples are soft but not completely collapsing – it's nice to have some larger pieces of apple too, so don't cook them for so long that they become a smooth purée.

Mix the cornflour to a paste with 1 teaspoon cold water and stir it through the apples, then simmer for another minute or so until slightly thickened, stirring. Turn off the heat and leave to cool completely – spreading the cooked apples out into a shallow dish will speed up this process considerably.

Once the apples are cold, preheat the oven to 200°C/180°C fan/gas 6, and place a heavy baking sheet in the oven to heat up.

On a lightly floured work surface, cut the pastry into 2 pieces, making one piece slightly larger than the other. Roll out the larger piece to a thickness of about 3mm and use it to line a deep pie plate (about 25cm in diameter) or a 23cm springform cake tin.

Transfer the cooked apples to the pastry case, levelling with a spoon. Brush the rim of the pastry with a little cold water. Roll out the other piece of pastry so it is slightly bigger than the top of the pie plate or tin and lay it over the filling, pressing down firmly onto the bottom piece of pastry to seal the edges. Trim the edges with a small sharp knife and then cut a couple of slits in the top of the pie to let the steam out. Brush all over with a little beaten egg or a mixture of milk and oil and sprinkle a little sugar over the top.

Slide the pie onto the hot baking sheet in the oven and bake for 40–50 minutes or until the pastry is deep golden brown and cooked through. Serve hot, warm or cold. I love apple pie simply served with cold cream, but many prefer ice cream or custard. This may be controversial to some, but if I serve custard on my pie, I serve it cold – for me it's the contrast in temperatures that works so well.

Tart Au Citron

An absolute classic among the sweet tarts, this version is truly lemony as I don't think this is the place for any half-heartedness. Lemon tarts in particular seem to be a little prone to cracking as they cool – I find that by leaving the tart in the tin as it cools you can minimise this problem. But cracks can still appear, and this is where the final dusting of icing sugar is very useful! As well as the more usual shortcrust, I sometimes make this with a polenta and almond pastry, which is crunchy and somehow pleasingly 'gritty', plus all importantly, it's gluten-free. See pages 11–12 for the recipe and tips on gluten-free pie baking.

Serves 6 | Takes 15 minutes to make (plus cooling and chilling), 30 minutes to cook

4 eggs
200g caster sugar
200ml double cream
**finely grated zest and juice of
 4 lemons**
**1 shallow 25cm blind-baked
 Shortcrust Pastry Tart Case
 (either made with standard
 Shortcrust Pastry, Sweet
 Shortcrust Pastry or Gluten-
 free Almond and Polenta
 Sweet Pastry – see pages 6–7
 and 11–12)**
icing sugar, for dusting

Preheat the oven to 180°C/160°C fan/gas 4.

In a large bowl, whisk together the eggs and caster sugar until they are well combined and slightly thickened. Add the cream and lemon zest and juice and whisk together well once more. Slowly pour the mixture into the pastry tart case and then slide the pie into the oven – I suggest placing the pastry tart case in its tin on a baking sheet (before filling) to make this a little easier, as the tart case will be very full.

Bake for 25–30 minutes or until the custard is set with a slight wobble in the centre. Remove from the oven and leave to cool completely in the tin.

Once cold, chill in the fridge for an hour or two before serving. Carefully remove the tart from the tin and place it on a serving plate. Just before serving, sprinkle over a little icing sugar. A little cream to drizzle over for serving will be nice with this tart.

Pear and Chocolate Tart

Just like strawberries and cream, bananas and toffee, and apples and blackberries, pears and chocolate are one of those classic combinations that simply work. For this rich, chocolaty tart, I've used canned pears – they are so easy, and when they are canned in juice rather than syrup, I love them.

Serves 6–8 | Takes 25 minutes to make (plus chilling and cooling), 55 minutes to cook

For the chocolate pastry
160g plain flour, plus extra for dusting
20g cocoa powder
1 tbsp icing sugar
a pinch of fine salt
90g butter, diced
about 3 tbsp ice-cold water

For the filling
200g dark chocolate (70% cocoa solids), broken into pieces
150ml whipping cream
50ml milk
2 eggs
75g caster sugar
410g can pear halves in juice, drained

To make the pastry, put the flour, cocoa powder, icing sugar and salt into a food processor and pulse briefly until combined. Add the butter and pulse a few times until it resembles fine breadcrumbs. Gradually trickle in the ice-cold water and keep pulsing whilst you do so, until the mixture resembles rather dry overcooked scrambled eggs, stuck together in little lumps. Don't bring the mixture all the way together into a ball just yet as this will result in over-processing and a tough pastry. (If you prefer, you can make the pastry by hand, using the traditional rubbing-in method.)

Tip the pastry onto a sheet of cling film and now bring it together into a ball, working gently so you don't squeeze out all the air gaps – these will add a lightness and crumbliness to the cooked pastry. Wrap tightly and chill in the fridge for 30 minutes.

Preheat the oven to 200°C/180°C fan/gas 6.

On a lightly floured work surface, roll out the pastry to a thickness of about 3mm and use it to line a shallow, fluted loose-based tart tin (about 25cm diameter), pressing well into the base and up the sides of the tin and making sure it fits snugly into the corners. Take the rolling pin and give it a swift roll across the top of the tin, neatly trimming off the excess pastry, then pinch around with your thumb and forefinger to squeeze the pastry just a little higher than the top of the tin (a couple of millimetres or so) – this will allow for a little shrinkage as it cooks and creates a nice neat finish.

Slide the tin onto a baking sheet and line with non-stick baking paper and baking beans (see page 10 for more tips on blind-baking). Bake in the oven for 20 minutes. Remove the paper and beans, then bake for a further 5 minutes to cook the pastry through completely. Remove from the oven and set aside.

Reduce the oven temperature to 180°C/160°C fan/gas 4.

Meanwhile, make the filling. Put the chocolate, cream and milk into a heatproof bowl and set the bowl over a pan of barely simmering water (making sure the base of the bowl doesn't come into contact with the water underneath). Stir from time to time until the ingredients are melted and combined and you have a glossy sauce – this will take around 5 minutes. Remove from the heat.

Break the eggs into a separate bowl, add the caster sugar and light beat together until slightly thickened. Add the chocolate and cream mixture to the egg mixture and beat together until well combined. Pour into the baked pastry case. Cut each pear half into 3 wedges and arrange over the chocolate filling, allowing them to sink down a little.

Bake in the oven for around 25–30 minutes or until the top is just set but with a slight wobble in the centre. Remove from the oven and leave to cool completely, then chill before serving, if you like. Carefully remove the tart from the tin and transfer it to a serving plate. Serve on its own or with a drizzle of cream.

Lemon Meringue Pie

The men in my family all seem to love lemon meringue pie, and both my brother and my son happily declare this to be their all-time favourite pudding in the world. I'm pretty partial to a slice myself to be honest – light-as-a-cloud meringue that is soft and squidgy inside, but with a little crunch as you bite through the surface, a tart super-lemony filling and a buttery crisp pastry case on the bottom. What's not to like?!

Serves 6 (but less in our family!) | Takes 25 minutes to make (plus cooling), 50 minutes to cook

For the filling and pastry tart case

5 tbsp cornflour
100g caster sugar
finely grated zest and juice of 4 lemons
80g butter, cut into 1cm cubes
4 egg yolks
1 deep 25cm blind-baked Shortcrust Pastry Tart Case (see pages 6–7)

For the meringue topping

4 egg whites
225g caster sugar

For the filling, measure 500ml cold water into a jug. Put the cornflour and sugar into a large mixing bowl, then pour in a little of the water – just enough to make a thick paste. Set aside. Pour the rest of the water into a saucepan and add the lemon zest and juice. Bring to the boil over a medium heat, then simmer steadily for a couple of minutes. Remove from the heat and gradually pour the hot lemon water over the cornflour and sugar paste, stirring constantly as you pour. Once the mixture is smooth and combined, pour it back into the pan, set over a low heat and simmer for a few minutes until thick and smooth, stirring.

Remove from the heat and stir through the butter and egg yolks, until well combined. Pour into the pastry tart case and level with the flat of a table knife or palette knife, then set aside to cool completely.

Once the lemon filling is cold, preheat the oven to 160°C/140°C fan/gas 3.

To make the meringue topping, put the egg whites into a squeaky-clean bowl and whisk until they hold soft peaks. A hand-held electric whisk or freestanding food mixer are ideal tools for this – a balloon whisk will do the job at a push, but it will be quite energy-consuming. Add the sugar, a third at a time, whisking really well between each addition until you have a thick and glossy meringue.

Spoon the meringue over the lemon filling, levelling it with the flat of a table knife or palette knife and making sure it reaches the pastry edges to cover the filling completely. Finish the top with a few artistic swirls.

Bake in the oven for around 35 minutes – after which time the meringue should be a light golden brown colour with a crisp surface. Remove from the oven and leave to go completely cold before serving. Carefully remove the pie from the tin and place it on a serving plate. This pie is perfect just served on its own.

Banoffee Pies

A truly indulgent sweet treat, these are best served in small quantities, so I like to make banoffee pies as little individual puddings. Or if you prefer, you can use this recipe and make one large quiche-size pie (about 25cm diameter) for sharing (you'll then need to increase the cooking time for the base by 5–10 minutes).

Makes 6 individual pies | Takes 25 minutes to make (plus cooling and chilling), 20 minutes to cook

For the base
175g digestive biscuits
80g pecan nuts
70g butter, melted

For the caramel sauce
100g butter
100g dark soft brown sugar
397g can condensed milk
$\frac{1}{2}$ tsp vanilla extract

For the topping
2 large bananas or 3 smaller ones
300ml whipping cream
a little dark chocolate, for grating

Preheat the oven to 200°C/180°C fan/gas 6. Grease and base-line 6 individual shallow fluted loose-based tartlet tins (each about 10cm diameter) with non-stick baking paper. Set aside.

For the base, put the biscuits and pecans into a food processor and whizz together to form fine crumbs. Add the melted butter and whizz again until combined. Divide the buttery crumb mixture evenly between the tins and press down firmly over the bases with the back of a spoon.

Bake in the oven for 10 minutes. Remove from the oven and leave to cool completely, then chill in the fridge for 30 minutes.

Meanwhile, to make the caramel sauce, put the butter and sugar into a small saucepan and set over a medium heat to melt and combine, stirring well. Pour in the condensed milk and add the vanilla extract. Bring up to the boil, stirring continuously, then boil for a couple of minutes or so until you have a thick golden caramel sauce. Remove from the heat and set aside to cool completely – pouring the mixture into a shallow dish will speed this up considerably.

When you are ready to serve, line up 6 small serving plates, then place $\frac{1}{2}$ teaspoon of caramel sauce into the centre of each. Carefully remove each biscuit pie base from its tin and place on top of the caramel to stick it down (this makes spreading the topping over much easier). Spoon a generous tablespoonful of caramel sauce over each biscuit base, spreading it out with a palette knife.

To prepare the topping and finish the desserts, peel and slice the bananas, then top each caramel-topped base with slices of banana. Whip the cream in a bowl until it forms soft peaks and then spread it over the bananas, dividing it evenly between the pies. Finally, grate a little dark chocolate over each pie to decorate.

Serve immediately or chill until needed – these pies are best eaten within 12 hours of making, as the bananas will soften and discolour over time. Served simply on their own is the best way with these pies.

Key Lime Pie

Some may feel this is a little borderline within the true definition of a pie, but it's called a 'pie', and it is delicious, so I feel entirely justified in including it here. I guarantee this will be the zestiest key lime pie you'll ever have tasted – I think if you are making a lime-flavoured pie it simply has to pack a mighty citrus punch. It's such an easy but impressive dessert – you simply chuck it all into a food processor and it's an absolute breeze.

Serves 8–10 (depending on greed) | Takes 15 minutes to make (plus cooling and chilling), 35 minutes to cook

For the base
225g digestive biscuits
110g butter, melted

For the filling
**finely grated zest and juice of
    5 fat limes**
4 egg yolks
200ml double cream
**397g can sweetened
    condensed milk**

Preheat the oven to 200°C/180°C fan/gas 6. Grease a 23cm springform cake tin and line the base with non-stick baking paper.

To make the base, put the digestives into a food processor and whizz to form fine crumbs. Pour in the melted butter and whizz again to mix. Tip the buttery crumbs into the bottom of the prepared springform cake tin and, using your hands, press the crumbs firmly all over the base and up the sides. Place the tin on a baking sheet to make transfer a little easier and bake in the oven for 10 minutes.

Whilst the base is in the oven, prepare the filling. Wash and dry the food processor bowl, then add the lime zest and juice to the bowl, along with the egg yolks, cream and condensed milk. Whizz together for a generous minute or so to ensure everything is completely combined.

Remove the base from the oven and reduce the oven temperature to 160°C/140°C fan/gas 3, leaving the door ajar for a few seconds to speed up the process. Pour the filling into the tin over the base, spreading it evenly, and then return it to the oven, taking care not to slop any filling over the sides as it will be quite liquid at this stage.

Bake for around 25 minutes or until the filling is just set with a little wobble in the centre. Remove from the oven and leave to cool to room temperature on a wire rack, then transfer the pie to the fridge and chill for at least 2 hours before serving.

Slide a blunt knife around the inside edge of the tin and release the springform, then carefully transfer the pie to a serving plate. Serve with a drizzle of cold double cream for extra richness, if you like, but it is lovely just served on its own (I prefer it served simply as it is).

Summer Strawberry Tartlets

Now this is my idea of the perfect sweet treat. Give me a dessert laden with fruit and creamy custard over a chocolaty one any day. Apologies if this sounds overly fussy, but I suggest that you only consider making these tartlets when British strawberries are at their peak, as they are absolutely the whole point of this recipe. Make them with watery out-of-season fruit and you will surely be disappointed. These tartlets are best eaten on the day they are made so the pastry stays nice and crisp.

Makes 6 individual tartlets | Takes 25 minutes to make (plus chilling and cooling), 20 minutes to cook

plain flour, for dusting
1 batch of Sweet Shortcrust Pastry (see pages 6–7)
3 egg yolks
45g caster sugar
25g cornflour
275ml milk
1/2 tsp best quality vanilla extract
250g ripe strawberries (ideally small ones), hulled
4 tsp redcurrant jelly

Lightly dust some flour over the work surface and cut the pastry into 6 equal-size pieces, gently rolling each piece into a ball. Roll out each ball to a thickness of about 3mm and use it to line an individual shallow fluted loose-based tartlet tin (about 10cm diameter), pressing well into the base and up the sides of the tin and making sure it fits snugly into the corners. Take the rolling pin and give it a swift roll across the top of each tin, neatly trimming off the excess pastry, then pinch around with your thumb and forefinger to squeeze the pastry just a little higher than the top of the tins (a couple of millimetres or so) – this will allow for a little shrinkage as it cooks and creates a nice neat finish. Chill in the fridge for 20 minutes.

Meanwhile, preheat the oven to 200°C/180°C fan/gas 6.

Slide the tins onto a baking sheet and line each one with non-stick baking paper and baking beans (see page 10 for more tips on blind-baking). Bake in the oven for 15 minutes. Remove the paper and beans, then bake for a further 5 minutes to cook the pastry through completely. Remove from the oven and leave to cool completely.

Whilst the pastry is cooking, make the crème pâtissière. Whisk the egg yolks and sugar together in a bowl until thick and creamy. Whisk in the cornflour and set aside. Pour the milk into a pan, add the vanilla extract and bring gently to boiling point. Pour the hot milk over the egg and sugar mixture, whisking continuously until completely combined. Pour the mixture back into the pan and set over a very low heat, stirring continuously until the custard thickens. Remove from the heat, pour into a heatproof bowl and press a layer of cling film onto the surface to prevent a skin forming. Set aside to cool completely.

Carefully remove the baked tartlet cases from the tins. Spoon the cold crème pâtissière into the pastry cases, dividing evenly. Arrange the strawberries on top, leaving them whole if they are small or cutting them in half if they are large. Warm the redcurrant jelly in a microwaveable bowl on High for just a few seconds, or in a small saucepan, until it is liquid. Brush over the strawberries to glaze them and then set aside for a few minutes to set. Serve cold. The only accompaniment these delicious tartlets might need is a perfect cup of coffee or tea, whichever is your favourite.

SWEET

Gooseberry and Almond Streusel Pie

I have a little gooseberry bush in my garden that just about seems to yield enough fruit for one recipe a year, so it has to be a special one! This year it was a luscious gooseberry pie – the soft sharp fruit nestled under a crunchy blanket of sweet, buttery, almond-studded topping. A pie I was thrilled with. Gooseberries are not the easiest of fruits to buy, so if you don't grow your own you may have to hunt them down. The good news is that the streusel pie treatment works brilliantly with all sorts of other fruit – try it with plums, greengages, raspberries or a classic apple and blackberry mix. Just adjust the ratio of sugar to suit the fruit's tartness. Gooseberries are sharp little devils so I am pretty generous with sugar in this recipe.

Serves 6–8 | Takes 20 minutes to make, 45 minutes to cook

plain flour, for dusting
1 batch of Sweet Shortcrust
   Pastry (see pages 6–7)
450g fresh gooseberries,
   topped and tailed, rinsed
75g granulated sugar
100g blanched whole almonds
100g plain flour
100g butter, diced
75g dark soft brown sugar

Preheat the oven to 200°C/180°C fan/gas 6, and place a heavy baking sheet in the oven to heat up.

On a lightly floured work surface, roll out the pastry to a thickness of about 3mm and use it to line a 23cm springform cake tin, bringing it about 4cm up the sides of the tin.

Scatter the slightly damp gooseberries evenly into the pastry case and then sprinkle over the granulated sugar, giving the tin a little shake from side to side to mix the sugar in a bit.

Put the blanched almonds into a food processor and blitz briefly to roughly chop. Add the flour, butter and brown sugar and pulse until you have rough crumbs. Alternatively, you can do this by hand – first, roughly chop the almonds, then rub the butter and flour together between your fingers and thumbs to make rough crumbs, and then stir through the chopped almonds and brown sugar.

Sprinkle the streusel topping evenly but gently over the gooseberries – don't pack it down too firmly otherwise it will lose its crumbly lightness. Slide the tin onto the hot baking sheet in the oven and bake for around 45 minutes or until the

pastry is cooked through and the gooseberries are soft and bubbling up through the topping.

Remove from the oven and leave to cool for a few minutes before sliding a knife around the inside edge of the tin and releasing the springform. Carefully transfer the pie to a serving plate or wooden board. My personal preference for eating this pie is to serve it at room temperature, with generous scoops of vanilla ice cream alongside. However, it can be served hot, warm or cold, with ice cream, cream or custard, whatever takes your fancy.

SWEET

Chocolate, Clove and Apricot Tart

The inspiration for this is two-fold – some clove-scented truffles I made for an Indonesian supper club I was running, and a wonderful recipe for a chocolate and apricot tart in the lovely Moro cookbook. I love cloves for their exotic musky flavour and this tart combines cloves, chocolate and apricots beautifully, to create this slightly unusual dessert.

Serves 8 | Takes 15 minutes to make (plus cooling), 45 minutes to cook

- 250g dried apricots, finely chopped
- 150g dark chocolate (ideally 70% cocoa solids), broken into squares
- 50g butter
- 1 tsp ground cloves
- 2 eggs
- 100g caster sugar
- 1 shallow 25cm blind-baked Shortcrust Pastry Tart Case (see pages 6–7)

Put the apricots into a saucepan, pour over 350ml cold water and set the pan over a medium heat. Bring to the boil, then reduce the heat a little and simmer steadily for around 10–15 minutes or until the apricot mixture is thick and soft. Remove from the heat and set aside to cool slightly.

Meanwhile, place the chocolate, butter and cloves in a heatproof bowl set over a pan of barely simmering water (making sure the base of the bowl does not come into contact with the water underneath). Stir regularly until melted and combined into a smooth sauce, then remove from the heat.

Preheat the oven to 200°C/180°C fan/gas 6.

In a mixing bowl, lightly whisk the eggs and sugar together. Add the melted chocolate mixture and lightly whisk together until combined.

Spoon the apricot mixture into the pastry tart case, spreading it evenly, then pour over the chocolate mixture.

Bake in the oven for around 30 minutes or until the filling is just set to the touch. Remove from the oven and leave to cool to room temperature before serving. Carefully remove the tart from the tin and transfer it to a serving plate. Serve warm or cold, with a dollop of crème fraîche.

Greengage and Ginger Strudels

I love greengages but I admit they can be hard to find – try hunting them down in a good greengrocer's in the late summer, or if you have a little space, plant your own tree (you can get great dwarf stock greengage trees that don't take up much room). Alternatively, if you are lucky enough to live in a fruit-growing area, check out local farmers' markets, market stalls or pick-your-own farms. If all else fails, deep purple plums make an excellent substitute.

Makes 2 strudels (each serving 3) | Takes 25 minutes to make, 35 minutes to cook

750g greengages, quartered and stones removed

75g caster sugar

75g (drained weight) stem ginger, drained and finely chopped

finely grated zest of 1 large orange

1 pack (250g) filo pastry (about 10 sheets)

50g butter, melted

2–3 tsp icing sugar, for dusting

Preheat the oven to 200°C/180°C fan/gas 6.

Put the greengages into a mixing bowl, then stir through the caster sugar, stem ginger and orange zest. Set aside.

Unroll the stack of filo pastry sheets onto the work surface. Lift up half of the pastry sheets (keeping them together in a stack), then cover the rest with a clean damp tea towel to prevent them drying out.

Take 1 sheet of filo (from the first stack) and brush it lightly with a little melted butter, then lay another sheet directly on top. Brush that sheet with a little melted butter and lay another sheet on top as before, then keep going in the same way, layering the sheets of filo on top of each other, until you have used all 5 sheets.

Lift the stack of filo pastry sheets onto a baking sheet and spoon half of the greengage mixture down the middle. Fold over one side to cover the fruit, brush the top of the folded pastry with a little more melted butter, then fold the other side over to seal the fruit filling inside, sticking it down onto the butter. Brush all over with a little more melted butter, then turn the short ends over, sticking them firmly down – you will be left with a large sausage roll shape with the fruit filling completely encased in pastry. Carefully roll it over so that the stuck edges are now all underneath and brush the top with a final slick of melted butter. Sprinkle evenly with a little icing sugar.

Repeat with the remaining sheets of filo pastry, melted butter, greengage mixture and icing sugar (assembling the strudel on a separate baking sheet) to make 2 separate strudels.

Bake both strudels in the oven for around 30–35 minutes or until cooked, crisp and golden. These strudels are best served immediately whilst the pastry is crisp and the filling bubbling. The pastry has a tendency to go a little soggy with time. A drizzle of cream or a dollop of natural Greek-style yogurt will be a great addition.

Salted Walnut Pies

These delicious pies are like little pecan pies but made with walnuts, which I prefer for their far more complex and interesting taste. A little salt added to the mix works absolute wonders to cut through the very intense sweetness.

Makes 6 individual pies |
Takes 20 minutes to make
(plus chilling and cooling),
40 minutes to cook

plain flour, for dusting
1 batch of Shortcrust Pastry
(see pages 6–7)
150g dark soft brown sugar
75g butter
75g golden syrup
1 tsp vanilla extract
$\frac{1}{2}$ tsp fine salt
2 eggs
150g walnut pieces, roughly
chopped

Lightly dust some flour over the work surface and cut the pastry into 6 equal-size pieces, gently rolling each one into a ball. Roll out each ball to a thickness of about 3mm and use it to line an individual shallow loose-based pie tin (about 10cm diameter), pressing well into the tin and making sure it fits snugly into the base and up the sides of the tin. Take the rolling pin and give it a swift roll across the top of each tin, neatly trimming off the excess pastry, then pinch around with your thumb and forefinger to squeeze the pastry just a little higher than the top of the tins (a couple of millimetres or so) – this will allow for a little shrinkage as it cooks and creates a nice neat finish. Chill in the fridge for 20 minutes.

Meanwhile, preheat the oven to 200°C/180°C fan/gas 6.

Place the tins on a baking sheet and line each one with non-stick baking paper and baking beans (see page 10 for more tips on blind-baking). Bake in the oven for 15 minutes. Remove the paper and beans, then bake for a further 5 minutes to cook the pastry through completely. Remove from the oven and set aside whilst you make the filling.

Put the sugar, butter, syrup, vanilla extract and salt into a small saucepan and set over a medium-low heat, then stir well for around 5 minutes or until the ingredients have melted and combined to form a smooth glossy sauce. Remove from the heat and leave to cool for around 10 minutes. Beat in the eggs, then stir through the walnuts. Divide the mixture equally between the cooked pastry cases, spreading it evenly.

Bake in the oven for around 13–15 minutes or until the filling is just set. Carefully remove the pies from the tins to serving plates and serve hot, warm or cold. These pies are perfect served just as they are, or serve with a drizzle of cream for an extra treat, if you like.

Mulled Plum Pie

Autumnal and comforting, this is a homely warming pie to bring out of the oven on a cold, wet, miserable evening. Suddenly life will feel just a little bit better – at least that's how food works for me and I wouldn't want it any other way.

Serves 4–6 | Takes 25 minutes to make (plus cooling), 1 hour 5 minutes to cook

150ml red wine
1 cinnamon stick
$\frac{1}{2}$ tsp whole cloves
800g plums, quartered and stones removed
75g granulated sugar
2 tsp cornflour
plain flour, for dusting
1 batch of Sweet Rough Puff Pastry (see pages 7–8)
1 egg, lightly beaten
1 tbsp caster sugar

Pour the red wine into a saucepan and add the spices, then bring to the boil and simmer steadily over a medium heat for 5 minutes to reduce. Stir through the plums and granulated sugar, then cover with a lid and simmer over a very low heat for a few minutes or until the juice runs from the plums. Remove the lid, turn up the heat a little and then simmer for about 10 minutes or until the plums are soft, stirring occasionally. In a small glass, mix the cornflour with 2 teaspoons cold water. Add to the plums, stirring constantly, and then simmer for a couple of minutes until the juices are thickened a little. Remove from the heat and leave to cool completely.

Once the plums are cold, fish out the cinnamon stick and as many cloves as you can find, but don't worry if you can't find them all. Preheat the oven to 220°C/200°C fan/gas 7 and place a heavy baking sheet in the oven to heat up.

On a lightly floured work surface, cut the pastry into 2 pieces, making one piece just a touch larger than the other. Roll out the larger piece to a thickness of about 3mm and use it to line the base of a deep 23–25cm pie plate. Don't pull and stretch the pastry into place but lift it gently and ease it into the plate – this will help to minimise shrinkage when it's cooking. Trim around the edges using a small sharp knife and brush the rim all over with beaten egg. Spoon the plum filling into

the pie plate, mounding it into the centre.

Roll out the other piece of pastry so that it's slightly bigger than the top of the pie plate and gently lay it over the filling, tucking it around the pile of fruit and pressing down firmly on the rim to seal the edges together. Trim around the edges with a small sharp knife and then, using your thumbs, crimp all around the edge to ensure the filling can't escape. Brush all over with beaten egg, sprinkle over the caster sugar, then cut a couple of slits in the top of the pie to let the steam out.

Slide the pie onto the hot baking sheet in the oven and bake for around 45 minutes or until the pastry is crisp and deep golden. If the top crust is browning too much towards the end of cooking, cover it with a loose tent of foil. Serve hot or at room temperature with a generous drizzle of double cream.

Rhubarb and Orange Spring Puddings

I don't know if these are slightly pushing the boundaries of what is or is not a pie, but it's a delicious filling wrapped up in a case, albeit not a pastry one, so I feel justified in including it here. This is a version of that classic dessert, summer pudding, this one being filled with a spring-like compote of pink rhubarb. Because rhubarb is much paler than the traditional summer pudding mix of blackcurrants, raspberries and strawberries, these spring puddings are much more subtle in colour.

Makes 4 individual puddings | Takes 25 minutes to make (plus cooling and overnight chilling), 10 minutes to cook

400g pink (forced) rhubarb, washed, trimmed and cut into 2cm pieces
150g granulated sugar
finely grated zest and juice of 2 large oranges
30g butter, melted
about 8–10 thin slices white bread, crusts removed

Put the rhubarb, sugar and orange zest and juice into a saucepan and set over a medium-low heat. Cook for around 10 minutes or until the rhubarb is soft and collapsing but not completely mushy. You need there to be quite a generous amount of syrup to soak into the bread, so add a splash of water if it looks a little dry. Taste to check the sweetness, adding a little more sugar if it's too tart. Remove from the heat and set aside to cool completely.

When the rhubarb is cold, prepare the moulds. You will need 4 dariole moulds, each about 8.5cm diameter and 5.5cm deep. Brush all over the insides of the moulds with the melted butter. Cut out 8 discs from the slices of bread, 4 smaller ones to fit the bottom of each mould and 4 larger ones to fit the top of each mould, then cut the remaining bread into strips that are the height of the moulds.

Press a bottom (smaller) disc of bread down into each mould, then use the bread strips to line the moulds all the way round the sides, very slightly overlapping them so there are no gaps. Divide the rhubarb mixture evenly between the moulds, packing it down and pouring in as much juice as possible. Finally, top each with a larger disc of bread,

pressing it down firmly. Wrap each mould tightly in cling film and put a weight (a small jar is ideal) on top of each. Chill in the fridge for at least 6 hours or preferably overnight.

When you are ready to serve, remove and discard the cling film and run a table knife all around the inside edge of each mould to release the puddings from the moulds. Place a small serving plate on top of each one and invert, giving the underside of the mould a sharp tap to help the pudding slide out. Serve fridge-cold with a drizzle of double cream.

Apple and Blackcurrant Suet Pudding

Suet crust pastry is really easy to make by hand, and as it steams the little nuggets of fat melt into the flour giving it a light texture. The filling here is made from apples and blackcurrants, but the blackcurrants can just as easily be plump blackberries if they are available and if you prefer them. This is just the sort of dessert that is most cheering on one of those days in summer when the weather is way too chilly and very disappointing – you know the days I mean, the ones when we feel like emigrating!

Serves 6 | Takes 30 minutes to make, 2 hours to cook

For the filling
125g granulated sugar
2 tsp cornflour
650g cooking apples
100g fresh blackcurrants

For the suet crust pastry
a little butter, for greasing
300g self-raising flour, plus a little extra for dusting
150g shredded beef or vegetable suet
25g caster sugar
12–13 tbsp ice-cold water

Prepare the filling by stirring together the granulated sugar and cornflour in a mixing bowl. Peel, core and chop the apples into 1cm pieces, dropping them into the sugar/cornflour mixture as you go, and giving them a little stir to coat every now and then. Once all the apples are in, lightly stir through the blackcurrants and then cover and set aside at room temperature whilst you make the pastry.

To make the suet crust pastry, first, grease a 1.2 litre pudding basin well with butter and set aside. In a large mixing bowl, mix the flour, suet and caster sugar together until evenly mixed. Add the ice-cold water, a spoonful at a time, until the dough comes together in a rough ball with very little loose flour left. Suet crust pastry takes a lot more water than regular shortcrust pastry so keep trickling in as much as you need. Use your hands to bring it together into a ball, mopping up any excess flour as you do so, and then tip it onto the work surface. Knead gently for a couple of minutes until smooth and quite elastic.

Lightly dust the work surface with a little more flour and roll out the pastry to a thickness of about 5mm. Use it to line the prepared pudding basin, pressing the pastry well into the bottom and up the sides of the basin, then trim off most of the excess around the rim, leaving a 1cm overhang.

Tip the fruit filling into the pastry-lined basin, packing it down as tightly as you can without breaking the pastry. It may come up a little proud at the top, but don't worry as it will reduce down slightly during cooking. To make the pastry lid, re-roll the pastry trimmings to form a 5mm-thick circle that is a little larger than the top of the bowl. Brush a little cold water on the top edges of the pastry in the basin, gently lay the pastry circle over the filling, then fold the overhanging pastry over the edge of the pastry lid. Press down firmly all around the edges to seal the top lid to the sides.

Cover the top of the basin with a piece of non-stick baking paper, securing it tightly with string, then cover this with a snug-fitting piece of foil. Lower the pudding into a large saucepan, resting the bottom on an upturned saucer to keep it from directly touching the heat. Pour enough boiling water into the pan so that it comes about halfway up the sides of the basin. Bring to a steady simmer. Cover tightly with a lid and steam for 2 hours, checking the water level once or twice and topping it up, if necessary.

Remove from the heat and carefully remove the basin from the pan. Unwrap and slide a blunt knife around the inside edge of the basin to loosen the pudding, then carefully invert it onto a serving plate. Serve immediately whilst piping hot. Serve this pudding with lots of custard.

Raisin and Whisky Tart

Packed full of whisky-soaked fruit, this tart is almost Christmassy in its richness, and a little certainly goes a long way. I have a vague memory of eating something similar for school dinners, minus the whisky, of course!

Serves 8 | Takes 15 minutes to make (plus overnight soaking and cooling), 30 minutes to cook

300g raisins
4 tbsp whisky
150g butter, softened to room temperature
100g dark muscovado sugar
2 eggs
finely grated zest of 1 lemon
1 shallow 25cm blind-baked Shortcrust Pastry Tart Case (see pages 6–7)

Put the raisins into a mixing bowl and pour over the whisky, stirring well to mix. Cover with cling film and leave to soak at room temperature, preferably overnight or for at least 2 hours. If you are short of time, gently warm the whisky and raisins together in a small saucepan to speed up the process, remove from the heat and then leave to soak for as long as you can.

Preheat the oven to 200°C/180°C fan/gas 6.

Put the butter and sugar into a food processor and whizz together until smooth and creamy. Add the eggs and lemon zest and whizz until smooth. (You can also do this by hand in a mixing bowl with a wooden spoon and a bit of elbow grease, or with a freestanding food mixer if you have one.) Transfer the mixture to a bowl, then add the whisky-soaked raisins and stir well until thoroughly mixed. Pour into the pastry tart case and spread it evenly.

Bake in the oven for about 30 minutes or until the filling is set and the surface has developed a slightly sugary crust. Remove from the oven and leave to cool completely in the tin. Carefully remove the tart from the tin to a serving plate and serve cold on its own or with a drizzle of thick double cream.

This tart keeps well for several days, stored in an airtight container or on a plate well wrapped in foil, at room temperature.

INDEX